Happy reading!
Vicky Nemethy
11-17-91

On the Banks of the Ole St. Joe

A Selected History
of
St. Joseph and Benton Harbor, Michigan

Author and Coordinator: Kathryn Schultz Zerler

Editing Supervisor: Peggy Lyons Farrington

Cover Designer and Illustrator: Vicky Nemethy

Contributing Writers: Harold A. Atwood, Rev. Christopher Momany, Jane Ammeson, Edward Conrad, Barbara G. Troost

Photographs courtesy of: St. Joseph Today, Roberta Drake Terrill, Maud Preston Palenske Memorial Library, Fort Miami Heritage Society

Sales Consultant: Jennifer Schanze

Publisher: St. Joseph Today

CONTENTS

Foreword

I am most pleased to share my personal enthusiasm for *On the Banks of the Ole St. Joe* and to express my thoughts on why I consider the concepts and ideals expressed herein so important to our community's heritage.

This is the first historical account written on the twin cities of St. Joseph and Benton Harbor for the 20th century. The book starts with our early history and traces the tremendous growth that has taken us into the 1990s.

I moved to this area 56 years ago as a young lad of six. I have witnessed many significant changes in the twin cities area and I can see emerging growth patterns that will improve our community for the future.

This book brings into focus memories of a heritage marked with the emphatic enthusiasm of our business leaders and other selfless residents who made the twin cities what it is today. Our current business leaders and the volunteers of many local organizations continue to strive to make this a better place to live and enjoy the natural beauties we abundantly share with each other.

I am confident that as you read through this very interesting story you will be encouraged to make this a special place in your life to love and share with others.

Edward J. Conrad
Executive Vice President
Twin Cities Area Chamber of Commerce

Preface

This project began in late 1984 when I was approached by several people who felt there was a need for a twentieth century history book about St. Joseph and Benton Harbor. Notably among these was Jean Spelman who had just stepped down as the executive secretary for the Fort Miami Heritage Society.

At that time I had no intention of writing the book myself, but launched a campaign to search for a writer. Barbara Troost, an assistant at the Maud Preston Palenske Memorial Library, had been asking people for years to tackle the same project to help round out the Michigan history section of the library.

Our mutual interest became the basis for this book. The decision was augmented by the passion for history found among local citizens.

Special thanks go to those who helped write the first walking tour for St. Joseph Today, including William and Mickey Campbell, then Mayor Franklin Smith, Gwenn Schadler, Mike Yore, Collins Gillespie, Robert Gillespie, current Mayor William Gillespie, Ruth Gillespie Grootendorst, Frank Lahr, Polly Preston Parrett, Nick State, Barbara Willey, Victoria Boothby, Rosalie Kimmerly, Patrick McMullen, Beverly Grose, Karen Pearson Johnson, Pearl Wilcox, Mary Pielemeier, A. G. "Pete" Preston, Jr., Jean Spelman, Herb Gorr, Phyllis Thurkettle, former Mayor Clifford Emlong, Rebecca Cooper and Michele Spencer.

It was challenging to keep up with the stories—some of them unprintable—that this group shared in the confines of the

St. Joseph Today office! The original tour subsequently became a popular brochure and a version is included as Chapter Ten of this book.

For the remaining chapters, we simply wanted to research and write them. This book is by no means the beginning or the end of twentieth century history about our communities. Our choice of content has been subjective with a focus on downtown St. Joseph, the site of the original explorations of what has since become an area comprised of two cities and five townships.

There are many stories left untold. We invite other writers to explore areas such as manufacturing, educational systems, small businesses and the many community leaders who have made the area successful.

In our writing we have striven for accuracy and in this attempt we owe grateful thanks to Glenn Zerler, Edward Conrad, Peggy Farrington, Mary C. "Lee" Passaro, Elizabeth Landis, Vicky Nemethy, Carol Weller, Phyllis Dowsett, Dar Davis, Roberta Drake Terrill, James Pomeroy, Michele Spencer, Kay Delle Koch, Christopher Momany, Jane Ammeson, Tom Lyons, and Jean and John "Jack" Spelman. For technical assistance we appreciate the extra efforts of Alicia Coard, Customer Service Representative at Imperial Printing Company.

Special thanks are extended to Richard Schanze whose financial advice and constant encouragement made publication of this book possible.

A special acknowledgment also goes to Harold A. Atwood for his painstaking writing of Chapter One on the early history of the twin cities. Due to his expertise, we have a first chapter which puts the remainder of our book in perspective. We also sincerely thank Tom Lyons, a long time resident of the area who read one of the early drafts and knew immediately that its title should be *On the Banks of the Ole St. Joe.*

For those readers who wish to delve further into local history, Barbara G. Troost has prepared the annotated bibliography to guide a search through the Maud Preston Palenske Memorial Library.

Kathryn Schultz Zerler
Executive Director of St. Joseph Today
from September 17, 1984 to the present

Aerial view shows the St. Joseph River running through the city of St. Joseph. Upper left corner shows part of the Morrison Channel.

Acknowledgments

Benjamin Franklin King, Jr.
March 17, 1857 to April 7, 1894

Throughout this book, chapters are prefaced with verses and poems by Ben King who is considered by many to be St. Joseph's most well-known poet. While little has been written about King's life, much can be surmised from his successful collection of poetry entitled *Ben King's Verse*.

The poems are witty comments on life as King observed it in the 19th century. He witnessed the early growth of St. Joseph and much of what he wrote then is still true. From his love of nature came rhymes about the St. Joseph and the Mississippi Rivers, pastoral odes about plants, animals and the four seasons. Included in his work is a generous sprinkling of verse inspired by the sun, the sea and the sky.

He often wrote in dialect, making wry statements about family and love relationships, the quest for money and power, and insightful—but gentle—jibes at human folly. His technique was broad enough in its appeal to earn him the honor of once being named the poet laureate of the Chicago Press Club.

King died an untimely death at age 37. He was mourned as a man who gave laughter and delight to many, and had so much more to give. He was buried by friends and relatives who considered him to be the "one who could least be spared from our circle."

The poems were copyrighted by his wife in 1894 and 1898; the first printing of Ben King's Verse came in August of 1898. The collection enjoyed 13 subsequent printings, the last in 1906.

His popularity was largely attributed to his talent for performing his poems while playing the piano, acting out both with humor that delighted audiences and reviewers alike.

John McGovern wrote this about King's performances in the introduction to the poetry book:

> He began as the expositor of "The Maiden's Prayer" on the piano, where each accented note was flat or sharp, and the music flowed rapidly or over great difficulties, as the score might determine. He arose, and looking half-witted, recited with inapproachable modesty the stammering delight which he would feel 'if he could

be by Her!' He frowsled his hair and became Paderewski, who forthwith fell upon the piano tooth and nail, tore up the track, derailed the symphony, went downstairs and shook the furnace, fainted at the pedals, and was carried out rigid by supers—the greatest pianist of any age. He wrote "If I Should Die To-night"— a parody that was accepted as the true original, the sun, the center of the great If-I-should-die-tonight system of thought and poetry.

For these humorous shows, King was favorably portrayed as a prophetic spirit in the newspapers. Considered a genius by his peers and close friends, his popularity grew. King was attaining a lauded reputation as a "mirthful shadow of conventional and tiresome things."

As an entertainer King toured the Midwest with Opie Read, a novelist and editor of the *Arkansas Travel*er. Read befriended King and later wrote a short biography on King which serves as a foreword to the poetry book.

With Read, King's performance fees were increasing along with his fame, when it all came to an abrupt end. After a successful show in Bowling Green, Kentucky, King was discovered dead in his hotel room.

Born on St. Patrick's Day in 1857 in St. Joseph, King was considered an odd child, understood by no one including his parents. He played the piano without benefit of lessons, and the eloquence of his music "startled his parents into the consciousness that a great talent had been given unto him."

He was a dreamer, often found lying on the banks of the St. Joseph River immersed in the sounds of birds, breezes and lapping water. In his teens, King moved to Chicago to pursue a career in poetry. To augment his income, he attempted to sell pianos on commission while writing and conducting poetry readings.

On November 27, 1883 King married Aseneth Belle Latham of St. Joseph. The wedding took place in Chicago, officiated by Professor David Swing. The Kings had two sons, Bennett Latham and Spencer P. King.

Thirty years after King's death, H. W. Gustin—a friend of King and a former St. Joseph postmaster—donated a bronze bust of King which was unveiled in 1924 in Lake Bluff Park before a crowd of some 200 admirers, including King's son Bennett. Sculpted by Leonard Crunelle of Chicago, the bust and pedestal cost approximately $1,000.

Inscribed on the pedestal is a verse from King's poem entitled "The River St. Joe:"

> "Where the bumble bee sips and
> the clover's in bloom
> And the zephyrs come laden
> with peachblow perfume.
> Where the thistledown pauses
> in search of the rose
> And the myrtle and woodbine
> and the wild ivy grows.
> Oh, give me the spot that I once
> used to know
> By the side of the placid old
> river St. Joe!"

Chapter

One

"Do you remember, Tom, Billy and Sal,
The old swimmin' days in the Bung Town Canal?
The big millin' logs fast asleep on its banks,
We used to jump off of and cut up odd pranks
In our tropical costume. We used to make Sal
Go home when we swum in the Bung Town Canal."

Verse from "The Bung Town Canal"
by Ben King

A Brief History of the Twin Cities
by Harold A. Atwood

Father Jacques Marquette, after establishing a mission in the Illinois country, may have been the first European to pass through this area. It is believed that Marquette, overtaken by illness, ascended the Illinois and Kankakee Rivers, portaged to the St. Joseph River, descended to its mouth, and then traveled north to a point near Ludington where he died. He named the local river after the Miami Indians who were living along its banks.

Four years later in 1679 the explorer LaSalle came to the site where the Whitcomb Tower now stands and built Fort Miami, while awaiting the arrival of the *Griffin*, first ship to ply the Great Lakes. When the ship vanished, LaSalle was forced to temporarily abandon his plans for further exploration of the Mississippi Valley and returned to Montreal. The 40' by 80' palisaded fort had a short history as it was abandoned after LaSalle planted the French flag at the mouth of the Mississippi in 1682.

When the ship vanished, LaSalle was forced to temporarily abandon his plans for further exploration.

After Montcalm's defeat at Quebec in 1759 control of this area passed into the hands of the British. After the American Revolution, all of the Great Lakes region south of present-day Canada became United States territory. About 1780 the William Burnett family arrived from New Jersey and established a trading post on the west bank of the St. Joseph River a short distance north of where the Napier Avenue bridge now stands. Prospering from the sale of furs and maple sugar, the family maintained the post until 1833.

In the fall of 1827, Captain Amos B. Hinkley was forced by a storm to take refuge in the St. Joseph harbor, and then found that he would have to spend the winter here. Hinkley and his crew built a log cabin and, as they waited for spring, they became impressed with the opportunities here and planned to return.

Settlement of the area had begun in earnest.

Meanwhile, with the opening of the Erie Canal in 1825 and the signing of the Carey Mission Treaty in 1828, settlement of the area had begun in earnest. Among the first to arrive at St. Joseph was Major Calvin Britain who had been a teacher at the Carey Mission. Major Britain and August B. Newell platted a village and called it

Newberryport. Captain Hinkley may have named the village after Oliver Newberry, a prominent businessman with whom he worked. Hinkley built a warehouse and Newell built a hotel called the Mansion House on the former site of Fort Miami. Edward P. Deacon and William McKaleb built a sawmill, and also built a steamboat, the *Matilda Barney,* which sailed up and down the river for about ten years. Thomas Fitzgerald arrived from New York, having been appointed keeper of the lighthouse located north of where the Curious Kids' Museum now stands at 415 Lake Boulevard, St. Joseph.

Major Britain and August B. Newell platted a village and called it Newberryport.

The village grew so rapidly that it was incorporated in 1834 and renamed St. Joseph after the river which the French had named for the patron saint of Canada. Fitzgerald became the first village president. In 1836, E. A. Draper began publishing *The St. Joseph Herald.* The harbor was greatly improved as workmen began building the north pier. Each year thereafter, hundreds of vessels entered the harbor to be loaded with fruit, grain, lumber and fish.

The village grew so rapidly that it was incorporated in 1834 and renamed St. Joseph.

The Territorial Road between Detroit and St. Joseph was opened in 1835. Two years later, Benton township was organized and named for Missouri Senator Thomas Hart Benton. The first town meetings were held at Millburg which had been laid out as a village as the Territorial Road came through. Eleazar Morton arrived at Saint Joseph in 1835 and purchased 160 acres of land east of the river. The next year, he moved his family into a log house on high ground west of Ox Creek, a site located in the middle of present-day East Main Street opposite the new Transportation Building at 275 East Wall Street, Benton Harbor.

Farmers who had settled farther east were bringing their produce to the harbor via Territorial Road. Upon reaching present-day Fifth Street, they followed a trail below the bluff south to Spink's Bridge and crossed the river where an island made bridge construction easier and less expensive. A trail along the west bank of the river led to the harbor.

The Morton place became a convenient rest stop for travelers to and from St. Joseph.

The round trip from Morton's house to the harbor often took a day. Thus, the Morton place became a convenient rest stop for travelers to and from St. Joseph. After one year Morton enlarged his house to provide for overnight guests and became a tavern keeper.

Morton and his son, Henry, set out a peach orchard and sold their first crop to Captain Curtin Boughton in 1841 for one dollar per bushel. Later, having expanded their holdings to 500 acres, they set out orchards consisting of apple, peach, pear, plum and apricot trees. In 1849 the Mortons moved into a new home which still stands at 501 Territorial, Benton Harbor. They continued to accommodate travelers in need of a place to stay. The Morton prosperity attracted the attention of others. In 1857 Messrs. Smith and Howell, representing a Cincinnati syndicate, rented seventy acres of land from Henry C. Morton. They set the entire tract to peach trees, and the "Cincinnati Orchard," producing 25,000 bushels of peaches per year, became known all over the United States.

...the "Cincinnati Orchard," producing 25,000 bushels of peaches per year, became known all over the United States.

Morton House in 1930.

Spink's Bridge was washed out by a flood. It was proposed that a new bridge be built at the west end of present-day Main Street.

A subscription drive was undertaken, and a road and bridge were built during the winter of 1858-59.

The Michigan Central, first railroad built across Berrien County, reached Niles in 1848 and New Buffalo in 1849. The economy of St. Joseph was adversely affected by this turn of events and village population actually declined. In 1858 Spink's Bridge was washed out by a flood. It was proposed that a new bridge be built at the west end of present-day Main Street. The project would be expensive because of the length of the span and the need for a three-quarter-mile long access road across the marsh. Henry C. Morton and Charles Hull attended a meeting of St. Joseph businessmen to ask for help but none was offered. A subscription drive among Benton Township residents was undertaken, and a road and bridge were built during the winter of 1858-59.

The bridge episode caused Sterne Brunson to propose that residents east of the river begin immediately to build a ship canal through the marsh and establish a new town. At first Brunson was subjected to considerable ridicule but, in the spring of 1860, a canal committee (Sterne Brunson, Charles Hull and Henry C. Morton) entered into a contract with Martin Green, a dredge owner from Chicago, to begin construction. Again a subscription drive was undertaken to pay for the project. Many township residents hauled wood to fuel the steam dredge. After two years a mile-long canal was opened with the eastern edge of the turning basin at the town line dividing Benton and St. Joseph Townships.

After two years a mile-long canal was opened.

As canal dredging began, J. E. Miller, a civil engineer and associate of Martin Green, platted the dry land which lay below the bluffs. When the plat was recorded in 1863, the village was named Brunson Harbor to honor the man who was generally regarded as the "town father." Brunson Harbor grew rapidly as lots were sold and wooden buildings erected. Fred Spallinger opened a grocery store. E. B. Whiting built a two-story hotel and named it the American House. H. N. Peck and Company began making fruit packages. Joseph Bell opened a blacksmith shop, and his son John became the town's first physician.

Brunson Harbor grew rapidly as lots were sold and wooden buildings erected.

The American House at Main and Pipestone Streets in 1880.

In 1866 a petition for incorporation as a village was granted and an organizational meeting was held at the "Little White School." The village name was changed to Benton Harbor and Samuel McGuigan was elected its first president. The new village was approximately one mile square with the southern boundary at Britain Avenue. The eastern half of the village was situated in Benton Township and the western half in St. Joseph Township. In 1868 Leonard J. Merchant began publishing *The Palladium*. A telegraph line was completed between Niles and Benton Harbor, and James Stanley Morton served as the first operator.

The village name was changed to Benton Harbor.

The canal made Benton Harbor a lake port. Its banks were soon lined with saw mills and basket factories. In 1870, the Benton Harbor Fruit Market was founded at the city wharf. Farmers lined up on Sixth Street to bargain with fruit brokers. Ships were loading more than 300,000 packages of fruit per year. In 1880 J. H. Graham, J. S. Morton and others organized the Graham and Morton Transportation Company and began operating a daily line of steamers to Chicago.

The canal made Benton Harbor a lake port.

Farmers lined up on Sixth Street to bargain with fruit brokers.

A rail connection to St. Joseph opened in 1870 when the Chicago and Michigan Lake Shore Railroad began run-

ning south to New Buffalo. Mail which
had been delivered by stage from Niles
now arrived by rail. The next year the

Mail which had been delivered by stage now arrived by rail.

Produce going to market on Sixth Street in Benton Harbor in 1905.

Benton Harbor Fruit Market.

railroad crossed the river to Benton Harbor and tracks were laid to Coloma, Watervliet and beyond. This railroad, known after 1899 as the Pere Marquette, is now part of the Amtrak system. In 1878 Alexander H. Morrison erected a wooden ware factory on land which is now a large island upstream from the harbor turning basin. The Morrison Channel was opened apparently for the convenience of the factory.

In 1885 a street railway with horse-drawn cars began operating between Benton Harbor and St. Joseph. Four years later Kentucky Colonel William Worth Bean arrived at St. Joseph and proceeded immediately to organize the Benton Harbor & St. Joseph Electric Light Company. By 1892 the twin cities had an electrified street railway system. Dr. George J. Edgecumbe came to Benton Harbor and founded the "Little College on the Hill" in 1886. Benton Harbor College ranked among the best in the state, but declined after Edgecumbe's death in 1915 and later ceased to exist.

Benton Harbor property owners west of Colfax Avenue, located in St. Joseph Township, were paying higher taxes than property owners east of Colfax who were paying taxes to Benton Township. Incorporation of Benton Harbor

Morrison erected a wooden ware factory on land which is now a large island upstream from the harbor turning basin.

A street railway with horse-drawn cars began operating in Benton Harbor and St. Joseph.

Benton Harbor College ranked among the best in the state, but declined after Edgecumbe's death in 1915 and later ceased to exist.

as a city would remove the west side residents from St. Joseph Township with consequent loss of revenue to the township. Thus, the issue was joined: should the two villages be incorporated as one city or should separate cities be created? The choice of a new name for one city aroused much controversy. Many Benton Harbor residents, fearful of losing their identity, campaigned for incorporation as a separate city. Residents in St. Joseph also opposed consolidation and changing the name of the village. In 1891 the state legislature decided to grant separate charters. The new city's boundaries

Should the two villages be incorporated as one city or should separate cities be created?

Benton Harbor College in the mid-1890s.

13

were moved south to Empire Avenue, east to Fair Avenue, and west to the river. Benton Harbor voters chose Fred A. Hobbs to be their first mayor.Dr. Luther I. McLin was the first mayor of St. Joseph.

Benton Harbor's first up-to-date hotel was built by Edward Brant at the northeast corner of Main and Water Streets. The three-story Hotel Benton could accommodate up to 200 guests at two dollars per day. At the southwest corner of Main and Pipestone Streets, the Jones and Sonner Block replaced the American House with stores and offices. In 1892 a new high school was built at Broadway and Colby Streets.

The three-story Hotel Benton could accommodate up to 200 guests at two dollars per day.

Benton Harbor High School at Broadway and Colby Streets.

Mercy Hospital was founded in 1897 by Dr. Henry V. Tutton. In 1896 the Yore Opera House, which had been built eleven years earlier at Sixth and Territorial Streets, was destroyed by a fire which took the lives of twelve twin cities firemen. The Bell Opera House, built in 1900 at Sixth and Wall Streets, survived until 1945 when it was declared not adaptable to movie viewing and demolished.

When Berrien County was organized in 1831, Niles was the county seat. It was moved to St. Joseph in 1832 and to Berrien Springs in 1837. After winning the support of Benton Harbor residents, St. Joseph regained the county seat in 1894. The present courthouse was com-

Mercy Hospital was founded in 1897 by Dr. Henry V. Tutton.

Mercy Hospital.

pleted in 1967 at a cost in excess of $1,000,000.

Huge numbers of tourists began coming to the area in the 1890s to escape the summer heat and relax on the sandy beaches or enjoy the inland rural scene.

Huge numbers of tourists began coming to the area in the 1890s to escape the summer heat and relax on the sandy beaches or enjoy the inland rural scene. In 1887 a mineral well was discovered in the northern part of Benton Harbor near the Paw Paw River. The water, believed to have health-giving properties, was piped to the Premier Hotel and Bath House which stood on the present site of the new Transportation Building. The four-story Plank's Tavern, later known as the Hotel St. Joseph, was built in 1889 near the harbor entrance. Two years later the Silver Beach amusement park was opened, and the Tabor Farm Resort began building summer cottages. Other popular resorts were: Eastman Springs (1880s), Emory's Farm and Resort (1890s), Higman Park (1900), and Manley's Resort (1908). In 1903 Benjamin and Mary Purnell established the Israelite House of David on a large tract of land east of Fair Avenue. Their amusement park attracted thousands of visitors. Jean Klock Park, a ninety-acre tract of land with about one-half mile of lake frontage, was given to the city of Benton Harbor in 1917 by Mr. and Mrs. J. N. Klock as a memorial to their daughter.

Interurban trains began running between St. Joseph and South Bend in 1906. Trains from Benton Harbor reached Dowagiac in 1911 and Watervliet in 1913. However, the coming of the automobile had devastating effects on earlier modes of transportation. Interurban trains stopped running from Benton Harbor in 1928 and from St. Joseph in 1934. In 1935 the twin cities street railway was replaced by buses.

Interurban trains began running between St. Joseph and South Bend in 1906.

As a new century approached industrialization was adding to the general prosperity of the two cities. In St. Joseph, the Truscott Boat Manufacturing Company was building launches and pleasure craft, the A. B. Morse Company had begun job printing, and Cooper, Wells and Company was knitting "iron clad" seamless hosiery in a factory popularly known as the "sock foundry" on the present site of Whirlpool Field. Fred and Louis Upton founded the Upton Machine Company, now Whirlpool, in 1911. James and Waldo Tiscornia and others founded the Auto Specialties Manufacturing Company in 1917, and Fred C. Palenske established the Industrial Rubber Goods Company in 1919. In 1905 the Benton Harbor Development Company was organized to attract industries to the city. Land grants and financial aid induced many industries to

As a new century approached industrialization was adding to the general prosperity of the two cities and Cooper, Wells and Company was knitting "iron clad" seamless hosiery in a factory popularly known as the "sock foundry" on the present site of Whirlpool Field.

locate here including: Baker-Vawter (1905), F. P. Rosback (1905), Covel (1907), Benton Harbor Malleable Foundry (1908), Crary Machine Works (1912), Saranac Machine (1913), and Superior Steel Castings (1916).

In Benton Harbor the 1920s were golden years, and a building boom reflected the prosperity of the times.

In Benton Harbor the 1920s were golden years, and a building boom reflected the prosperity of the times: Benton Harbor High School (1921), Liberty Theater (1922), Vincent Hotel (1925), Naval Reserve Armory (1926), Fidelity Building (1927), YMCA Building (1927), Eleanor Club (1928), and more, including a junior high school, five new churches and a synagogue.

St. Joseph saw construction of the YWCA Building (1925), the Whitcomb Hotel (1928), and more, including churches, schools and a new city hall. An annual blossom festival was begun in 1923, after a suggestion by Fred L. Granger was enthusiastically promoted by the Rev. Joshua O. Randall of the Methodist Peace Temple.

Annual sales at Benton Harbor Fruit Market exceeded $8,000,000.

The Benton Harbor Fruit Market was moved in 1930 to a 34-acre site at Ninth and Market Streets. Open from June to November, with sales exceeding $8,000,000 per year, it had by now become known as "the largest cash to grower non-citrus fruit market in the world." Trucks were now transporting fruit, and the historic ship canal was abandoned to allow for much needed parking space.

In 1934 St. Joseph celebrated its centennial, and in 1984 its sesquicentennial was observed with memorials placed in Lake Bluff Park. Benton Harbor's Filstrup Field was the setting for pageantry and fireworks during its centennial celebration in 1966. On each of these occasions, twin cities residents looked back with considerable satisfaction to the achievements of their founding fathers and succeeding generations.

Harold A. Atwood is a retired Benton Harbor High School teacher and local historian.

Chapter

Two

"There is an olden story,
'Tis a legend, so I'm told,
How the flowerets gave a banquet,
In the ivied days of old;
How the posies gave a party once
That wound up with a ball,
How they held it in a valley,
Down in Flowery Kingdom Hall."

Verse from "The Flowers' Ball"
by Ben King

Celebrating Agriculture:
The Blossomtime Festival

Signs of spring in St. Joseph and Benton Harbor include acres of budding orchards and hundreds of volunteers working on Blossomtime, one of the largest festivals honoring agriculture in the nation. Organizers call it "a celebration of life renewed."

The event attracts some 600 young women from 30 area communities who vie for the title of Miss Blossomtime, as well as an estimated quarter million spectators in attendance at the Grand Floral Parade. Held in the twin cities of St. Joseph and Benton Harbor, Blossomtime claims to be the oldest multi-community festival in Michigan.

It began in 1906 when Reverend W. J. Cady of the First Congregational Church in Benton Harbor sermonized that blossoms on local farms were a symbol of life renewed. He officially declared Blossom Sunday and urged everyone to drive through the orchards. That religious beginning is still observed today with the annual Blessing of the Blossoms.

Other settlers noticed the abundance of his crop and followed his lead and the area became known as The Fruit Belt.

William Burnett, an early settler here who built a trading post on the St. Joseph River in the 1780s, discovered the fertile soil and favorable climatic conditions when he planted an apple orchard on his land near the trading post. Other settlers noticed the abundance of his crop and followed his lead. In time, the area became known as The Fruit Belt, a 30-mile strip inland from Lake Michigan tempered by the lake.

The first recorded shipment of peaches was grown in south St. Joseph township and transported by boat to Chicago in 1830.

Loading fruit baskets in 1911.

Apricot petals are among the first to open. Plum, pear, crab apple, cherry, peach and apple trees are close behind. Mapped trails are available from the Southwest Michigan Tourist Council for excursions through the fragrant fields as are horse-drawn wagons to make the trip in traditional style.

"A walk through the orchards is like being inside a flower," says Michelle "Mickey" Bennett of Sodus, a rural village east of Benton Harbor. "The season is short, but it's worth the time to keep an eye on the orchards and ride out when they're in full bloom."

About half the private land in Michigan, 14 million acres, is used for agri-

Fruit buyers on the steps of the Benton Harbor Library in 1903.

culture which is one of the state's largest sources of income. Approximately 25 percent of Michigan's citizens derive all or part of their income from activities dependent on agriculture.

Religious leaders have always played an important role in what evolved into a week of Blossomtime festivities encouraging farming and related industries. Although Blossom Sunday was discontinued in 1917, Reverend Joshua O. Randall of the Methodist Peace Temple in Benton Harbor and Fred L. Granger, a local fruit processor, remembered the day and conceived the idea of a floral parade in 1923 to take its place. The two men secured further help in promoting the project from the Rotary Club, Exchange Club and the St. Joseph Chamber of Commerce.

In 1936 Granger recalled the events of 1923 in a letter to the editor of the local newspaper. He said, "Blossomtime was almost upon us, and the only publicity plan we were able to develop resulted in our hiring a big, new truck belonging to Wells-Buick Company, filling it with branches and blossoms from Friday Brothers' Orchards, and decorating the truck with large signs inviting the public to come to Blossomtime in Benton Harbor and St. Joseph, Michigan. This truck was transported to Chicago on the

Graham and Morton Line. Harry Meyering secured a permit from the police department in Chicago allowing us to circulate the truck 'round and 'round the Loop district for two days with its music inviting the people of Chicago to participate in nature's spectacle—our Blossom Festival. This is the history of the beginning of the present Blossom Festival, which you can confirm from your own records and that of the Rotary Club."

Harry secured a permit from the police department in Chicago allowing us to circulate the truck 'round and 'round the Loop district for two days with its music inviting the people of Chicago to participate in our Blossom Festival.

Kathryn Patrick and Polly Preston are seated at the front of this 1929 float by the Standard Oil Company. Anne Preston and Barbara Fowler are at the back.

The first parade was held on a Wednesday afternoon. The second parade, on May 14, 1924, had 30 floats, two marching bands and hundreds of private automobiles which made a tour of the new "Blossom Lanes" of southwestern Michigan. General chairman was Fred Granger, and the Benton Harbor Kiwanis Club won the sweepstakes award. These activities set patterns for the festivals for many years.

Benton Harbor fire truck float, The Heart of the Fruit Belt, on Market Street in St. Joseph.

In 1924 Miss Catherine Burrell of Benton Harbor was chosen by newspaper ballots to reign as the first Blossom Queen. In subsequent years communities held their own contests selecting queens to participate in a collective pageant for the title of Miss Blossomtime.

The festival was interrupted again in 1943 with the advent of World War II. In 1951 the St. Joseph and Benton Harbor Chamber of Commerce fostered the creation of Blossomtime, Inc., a non-profit organization of some 75 members governed by a board of directors. They held the first post-war festival in 1952. The Blossom Parade that year attracted about 150,000 spectators who watched 56 units. Among these was the first annual sweepstakes winning float entered by the House of David.

Stanley R. Banyon, *Herald-Press* and *News-Palladium* publisher, said this about the festival, "At the outset of World War II, it was decided that the Blossom Festival be temporarily suspended until after the allied forces had defeated the enemy. After the war there was public demand for the resumption of Blossom Week. It's a festival that focuses national attention on Michigan's famed Fruit Belt. The crowning event is the spectacular Blossom Parade. Over the years it has attracted millions of

It's a festival that focuses national attention on the famed Fruit Belt.

people from all over the heart of the Midwest. Blossom Week is actually the forerunner of almost a legion of similar festivals in many Michigan communities including the Tulip Festival in Holland and the Traverse City Cherry Festival. Southwestern Michigan is the fruit capitol of Michigan. Our Fruit Market in Benton Harbor is nationally known. From far and wide, and even from foreign shores, delegations have come to inspect the market and its operations."

Blossomtime Inc. became an independent non-profit entity separate from the

Whirlpool's 1987 float, Michigan's Musical Memories, won the Sweepstakes Award in the Grand Floral Parade

chamber in 1969. It runs the festival today as a volunteer organization governed by a twelve person board of directors and an executive director. The group works all year to produce a week of entertainment and events culminated by the Grand Floral Parade, also called the Blossom Parade.

Executive directors of record include Leo Issac from 1969 to 1970, Phyllis Taylor Dowsett 1971 to 1984 and Carol Weller 1984 to the present. The salaried position requires full-time, year-round work.

Held on the first Saturday in May at 1:00 p.m. the parade now lasts approximately two hours and has about 100 entries including floats, bands, comic groups and special units such as unicyclists, horse teams and jugglers. Participants come from Michigan, Illinois and Indiana as well as Wisconsin, Ohio and other states.

Carol Weller, Blossomtime's current executive director and a volunteer since 1974, is proud to be a part of it all. "I've worked in all areas of the festival. It's very busy and exciting. Last year I walked the whole parade route and talked to so many people who love the parade."

"We always go to the Blossom Parade, but I never get my chair there early enough."

Others agree about the excitement of the festival, especially the parade. "When I think about Blossomtime, I think of floats and kids in the bands," says Barb Bannow of St. Joseph. "We always go to the parade, but I never get my chair there early enough."

Children participate in Blossomtime with the Bud Prince and Princess Pageant and the annual Youth Parade. Other activities include a carnival, an author and celebrity reception, an arts and crafts fair, a run and a bicycle ride.

"People are what it's all about, that's the whole festival," says Linda Fites, a volunteer for eight years. "It gets in your blood, I suspect that's why it keeps going."

Doug Landis, owner of Landis Clothing Company near the parade route in downtown St. Joseph, agrees. "Business is pretty good on parade day. There's interesting people in town and that's why I'm in business—I like people," he said.

Ironically, at the time of the festival most farmers are too busy to enjoy it.

One family has traveled from Detroit for 12 years in a row for the parade. Ironically, at the time of the festival most farmers are too busy to enjoy it.

Alyce Jung, owner of Jung's Flower Farm in Benton Harbor, is representative of those farmers who support the Blossomtime festivities, but because of the nature of her business, is unable to participate. She says, "We used to go to the parade when the kids were small, but the first weekend in May is a very busy time for us. We're in the greenhouse moving flats and selling bedding plants." In fact, most of the spring and summer months are peak work times for growers, not to mention harvest time in the fall.

Here, in Blossomland, 52,000 acres of fruit crops with more than 3.3 million trees produce from 12 to 18 million bushels of apples, 20 to 25 million pounds of blueberries, 350 to 500 million pounds of cherries, 3.5 million bushels of peaches, 25,000 to 60,000 tons of grapes and tons of pears, plums, black raspberries and strawberries.

And there's more. A wide variety of flowers, vegetables and other fruits are grown in Michigan. All of these are regularly inspected by the Michigan Department of Agriculture for any residue from pesticides insuring that Michigan produce is a wholesome commodity.

In Blossomland, 52,000 acres of fruit crops with more than 3.3 million trees produce 12 to 18 million bushels of apples, 20 to 25 million pounds of blueberries, 350 to 500 million pounds of cherries, 3.5 million bushels of peaches, 25,000 to 60,000 tons of grapes and tons of pears, plums, black raspberries and strawberries.

*Many farmers
stock their irri-
gation ponds
with fish. Others
maintain the
lands around
their farms as a
natural habitat
for wildlife.*

Many farmers stock their irrigation ponds with fish. Others maintain the wooded lands around their farms as a natural habitat for wildlife. Streams and rivers are also monitored for chemical run-off with the results showing that heaviest concentrations are found in non-agricultural areas.

The twin cities of St. Joseph and Benton Harbor are located just off I-94 in the southwest corner of the state. They are a three-hour drive from Detroit and a two-hour drive from Chicago. The communities have miles of sandy beaches, many public golf courses, charter fishing, fine dining, wineries, river and big lake water sports and many other tourist attractions.

For more information, please call or write: Blossomtime, Inc., 151 East Napier, Benton Harbor, Michigan 49022, (616) 926-7397, or contact the Twin Cities Area Chamber of Commerce, (616) 925-0044; the Southwestern Michigan Tourist Council, (616) 925-6301; St. Joseph Today, (616) 982-6739.

Blossomtime Presidents

1951	Ray Jeffers
1952-54	Joe Carver
1955-56	Bert Lindenfeld
1957-58	Randall "Red" Burch
1959-63	Thomas Dewhirst
1964-65	Charles Knipschild
1966	Terry Baccash
1967-68	Vernon Schmaltz
1969	Robert Braamse
1970-71	Donald Humphrey
1972	Jay Holt
1973	Jim Barricklow
1974	Paul Florin
1975-76	Don Young
1977	William Starbuck
1978-79	Gertie Johnson
1980-81	David Fister
1982	Bud Dudas
1983	David Fister
1984	Gertie Johnson
1985	Dean Sanders
1986-87	Dr. George Schuster
1988-90	Susan Youdell

Bl.. .m Queens

1924 Catherine Burrell, Benton Harbor
1925 Ruth Miller, St. Joseph
1926 Gladyce Dempsey, Buchanan
1927 Violet Peters, Benton Harbor
1928 Elsie Lemke, St. Joseph
1929 Lilian Shepard, Battle Creek
1930 Cecelia Eisenhart, Buchanan
1931 Jane Filstrup, Benton Harbor
1932 Margery Noble Crampton, Grand Rapids
1933 Marion Evans, Berrien Springs
1934 Connie LeGard, Muskegon
1935 Marybeth Kemp, Battle Creek
1936 Virginia May Pound, Grand Rapids
1937 Alice Merson, South Haven
1938 Dorothy McBride, Kalamazoo
1939 Anna Belle Dykstra, Kalamazoo
1940 Joan Payne, Three Rivers
1941 Jean Muske, South Haven
1942 Marion Radke, St. Joseph
1952 Waiva Lenox, Buchanan
1953 Annette Miller, Benton Harbor
1954 Barbara Schoch, New Buffalo
1955 Patricia Hanley, Dowagiac
1956 Susan Camburn, Three Oaks
1957 Brenda Tait, South Haven
1958 Nancy Reiner, St. Joseph
1959 Nancy Strijc, Coloma
1960 Donna Jean Shepard, Dowagiac
1961 Beth Dall, Berrien Springs

1962 Carol Ann Bowerman, Niles
1963 Gerri Glidden, Mattawan
1964 Louann Delisle, Sodus
1965 Gail Frielink, Lawrence
1966 Martha Krause, Berrien Springs
1967 Pamela Assgaard, New Buffalo
1968 Eileen Heyn, Bridgman
1969 Carla Sherrill, Three Oaks
1970 Sandra Jane Grams, St. Joseph
1971 Katherine Reitz, Baroda
1972 Deborrah Knox, Edwardsburg
1973 Deborah Zemke, Bridgman
1974 Debra Lichnerowicz, Hartford
1975 Cynthia Thornburgh, Niles
1976 Kimberly Smith, Gobles
1977 Kathy Necas, Stevensville
1978 Sheri Lyon, Lawrence
1979 Kathy Hahn, Stevensville
1980 Lana Sue Thompson, New Troy
1981 Cara Ann Hankila, Buchanan
1982 Nina Marie Ritter, New Buffalo
1983 Kim Otto, Lawrence
1984 Bonnie Goldner, Sodus
1985 Diane Novacek, Three Oaks
1986 Shelle Wegner, Stevensville
1987 Jill Reimann, St. Joseph
1988 Lainie Howard, St. Joseph
1989 Julie Ann Starbuck, Baroda
1990 Sonya Mingo, Covert

Chapter

Three

"If I should die to-night
    And you should come to my cold corpse and say,
    Weeping and heartsick o'er my lifeless clay—
    If I should die to-night,
And you should come in deepest grief and woe—
And say: 'Here's that ten dollars that I owe,'
    I might arise in my large white cravat
    And say, 'What's that?'

    If I should die to-night
And you should come to my cold corpse and kneel,
Clasping my bier to show the grief you feel,
    I say, if I should die to-night
And you should come to me, and there and then
Just even hint 'bout payin' me that ten,
    I might rise the while,
    But I'd drop dead again."

"If I Should Die To-night"
by Ben King

The Whitcomb Hotel

Early hotels were rude affairs, according to L. Benjamin Reber in his book, *History of St. Joseph.* Built of logs, they were more like taverns than hotels. Often the kitchen and dining rooms were one, with hosts carving huge roasts of wild game and loaves of bread as guests called out—loudly—for more. Eating utensils were not used unless diners brought their own, instead, hunks of bread sopped up food from plates. "It was rude fare, rudely served," wrote Reber, "but there was probably more real enjoyment at meal time than there is in one of our modern hotels."

Eating utensils were not used unless diners brought their own, instead, hunks of bread sopped up food from plates.

The first hotel, on the Whitcomb site at 509 Ship Street in St. Joseph was a crude log structure known as the Mansion House. Built in 1831 by August Newell, the Mansion House functioned as a wayside inn for travelers on the Chicago to Detroit stagecoach and was used by fur trappers.

The Michigan House was constructed in 1834 below the bluff to accommodate river boatmen. The busy river spawned yet another hotel one block inland from the Mansion House on the northwest corner of Ship and State. Named the Perkins House, built in 1840, Reber called it "the most famous of the old hotels." Other hotels built during this time catered to farmers, lumbermen and ship builders as well as travelers. Among these were the Park Hotel and the National Hotel.

Capitalizing on their success, B. C. Hoyt constructed his hotel across the street from the Mansion House in 1867. Initially known as the Hoyt House, this inn would later become the Lakeview Hotel. Both places thrived in their locations on the corners of Ship and Lake Boulevard, overlooking the St. Joseph River and Lake Michigan.

His claim that the hotel was the biggest and most beautiful in the area failed to produce expected revenues. It closed in 1872.

In 1868 Charles Krieger, in competition with Hoyt, replaced the Mansion House with a larger establishment which he called the St. Charles. His claim that the hotel was the biggest and most beautiful in the area failed to produce expected revenues. The hotel closed in 1872, just four years after the rebuilding. It changed hands many times, becoming known as the Whitcomb sometime during the 1890s.

View of the Whitcomb and Lakeview hotels. Sign on Whitcomb reads "Whitcomb Mineral Baths Cure Rheumatism and all nervous diseases."

According to legend, this addition was built for a bath house after a well driller hit sulphur while drilling for drinking water. Left to right is the bath house, the Hotel Whitcomb, the Lakeview Hotel and the 505 Pleasant Street building.

When Mr. Whitcomb came to town, he was perceived as well educated, a stylish dresser and a fast talker.

When Mr. Whitcomb came to town, he was perceived as well educated, a stylish dresser and a fast talker. He is reputed to have been either a "drummer" (then a name for salesmen) or a steamship agent for the Detroit/Cleveland line.

Whitcomb installed mineral baths in the basement, filling them with sulphur water from wells drilled 820 feet below the hotel. This was the second attempt at a "health resort" in St. Joseph. The first mineral baths were installed in the Park Hotel which drew water from a 190 foot well. The Park was located on the site of today's Elks Club at 518 Broad Street.

The pungent water was said to have great therapeutic value.

The pungent water could be smelled for blocks around and was said to have great therapeutic value. Though the Park Hotel was unsuccessful, mineral baths made the Whitcomb famous, and the hotel was popular at the turn of the century and for two decades beyond.

Men were lowered into large bathtubs with straps and netting.

Men were lowered into large bathtubs with straps and netting. Women's facilities included Swedish cabinets. Some famous people who came for the Whitcomb baths were Eleanor Roosevelt, Ring Lardner, Marian Anderson and Duncan Hines.

44

"When Charles Lindberg was practicing for his Atlantic flight, he used to fly across the lake from Chicago and tip his wing when he'd go over the Whitcomb," said Marian (Stock) McKenna of St. Joseph, a daughter and granddaughter of the men who built the present day Whitcomb.

The hotel drew large crowds of tourists, especially from Chicago, who felt that the baths were beneficial for various diseases. According to Reber, "St. Joseph was known all over the country as a health resort."

"St. Joseph was known all over the country as a health resort."

This photograph of a Sunday or a holiday gathering was taken on Lake Boulevard at Ship Street across the street from the Whitcomb. The building at the left came to be called The 505 Building at 505 Pleasant Street. At the far left is part of a porch from the Lakeview Hotel. The sign on the telephone pole indicates a stop for the street railway and a notice that interurban connections for Tabor Farm may be made in Benton Harbor.

Despite its creden-
tials as the *place*
to go, the hotel shut
down again in
1926.

Despite its credentials as *the* place to go, the Whitcomb Hotel shut down again on November 11, 1926. An anonymous paper found in the public library read, "merchants were aghast realizing the loss of business and decline in stature of the town. They met and reached a conclusion that a new hotel could be built if the cost was kept within the means of the community. On November 19 a drive began with the cost estimated at one million dollars. Under the leadership of W. F. Murphy, the committee had pledges and cash of $251,000 by December 21, $275,000 by December 25, $331,000 by December 31, and another $69,000 in pledges. In the final analysis, there were 306 stockholders."

The hotel, as it stands today, was designed by Pond, Pond, Martin and Lloyd, a Chicago architectural firm whose credits include the University of Michigan Union building and the St. Joseph Congregational Church. Construction was done by M. W. Stock and Sons of St. Joseph.

"I was just a little
girl, but I remem-
ber the dedication
ceremony as being
quite elaborate."

"My grandfather and father built the Whitcomb," recalls Marian (Stock) McKenna. "I was just a little girl, but I remember the dedication ceremony as being quite elaborate."

According to her sister, Marjorie (Stock) Clemens, their mother had a new gown for the three nights of parties in honor of the new building. Marjorie still has the velvet wrap with white fox fur trim worn by Mrs. Stanley Stock. "I was more interested in the bricks and mortar than the parties," said Marjorie. "Construction was much different in those days. They didn't wear hard hats or have many safety catches. I remember climbing up the ladders and watching the men wet down the cement so it wouldn't dry out too fast."

"Construction was much different in those days. They didn't wear hard hats or have many safety catches."

A special edition of the *Herald-Press* said this about the ceremony, "The date was May 3, 1928 and inside the newly built Whitcomb Hotel four snowy-haired pioneer women unveiled a mural painting steeped in local history. The panel, depicting Father Marquette and explorer Joliet in birch bark canoes paddling the vast expanse of Lake Michigan, was the culmination of a dream of the four St. Joseph women and the women's Chamber of Commerce to present something of beauty and value to the city. Mrs. Kalterbourne, joined by Mrs. E. A. Graham, presented the mural along with Mrs. W. A. Preston, Mrs. Alonzo Vincent and Mrs. R. F. Stratton to Mayor L. A. King who in turn loaned it to the Hotel Whitcomb." This mural hangs in the Marquette Lounge today.

The hotel had 225 rooms overlooking either the lake, the river or the downtown. The dining room served 800, and the food service area included a freezer plant able to keep the ice boxes filled with up to 1500 pounds of ice a day—an important capability as there were separate boxes for vegetables and fruit, meat and poultry, dairy products, seafood and soda bar supplies.

Despite its singular grandeur, the hotel went bankrupt again just six years after the rebuilding.

Despite its singular grandeur, the Whitcomb Hotel went bankrupt again just six years after the rebuilding. It was immediately purchased by the First United Finance Company—owned by the Frieder family of Chicago—on February 7, 1934.

Company president, Edward Frieder, named his son-in-law, Leon J. Harris, managing director, and the Harris family moved into the Whitcomb in March of that year. Mrs. Leon (Irma Frieder) Harris said, "It was during the depression years that we came to St. Joseph. The hotel had been neglected and run-down. The walls of the lobby were black with dirt and the sulphur fumes from the bath department were being forced into the lobby."

The new owners redecorated the rooms which rented for $5 for twin beds with a lake view, single rooms for $3.50, and $2 for alley rooms. The Harris' had other improvements in mind, several which they implemented at once.

Mrs. Harris said, "Many times my husband had to go without his salary in order to pay the employees." Later, during more prosperous times, he would pay his employees in silver dollars instead of checks so the hotel's economic impact on the community could be clearly seen.

With the end of Prohibition, the Harris' hired an architect to design a bar in the basement which they named the Yacht Club. It became a popular watering hole known as the "Marine Bar." Built like a boat with a gang plank entrance, the bar featured foreign posters and steamer trunks. Building supports were disguised as funnels, and portholes were made of dark blue glass.

"The old 'Marine Bar' was the place to go," said Ruth (Gillespie) Grootendorst of St. Joseph. "There was always something going on." Her sentiment is shared by many residents.

A solarium equipped with 17 sunlamps, and a gymnasium were installed on the seventh floor. Artist Raymond Katz of New York City, painted murals on the walls. The lobby was improved with the

"Many times my husband had to go without his salary in order to pay the employees."

"The old 'Marine Bar' was the place to go."

addition of a cigar and gift shop. "We always had a woman salesperson in the shop," said Mrs. Harris. "We learned at one hotel meeting that men are lonely on the road and would rather talk to a woman."

Referred to as the patio today, the sunken room on the west side was enclosed with glass windows and used as a banquet room with seating for 400. "The outside terrace between this room and the lobby was covered with a skylight," said Mrs. Harris. "There were

Rendering of the Whitcomb Hotel during the 1940s.

tropical plants and white iron garden furniture on this level. The room was named the Tropical Room."

A sun deck was placed over the roof of this room and an aviary was added alongside to house colorful birds. The most famous of these was Polly Whitcomb, a notorious bird who perched in the lobby and would sing if there was a crowd of people. "Sometimes her falsetto singing would bother speakers in the Tropical Room, and she had to be moved to the dining room," said Mrs. Harris. "She loved to say 'Shut that door!'" Polly became famous when her kidnapping made the Chicago papers.

Polly Whitcomb was a notorious bird who perched in the lobby and would sing if there was a crowd of people.

Mrs. Harris named the main dining room the Calvin Britain Room after St. Joseph's first settler. The room was elegant with china, white Irish linen, fresh flowers, candlelight, carpeting and crystal chandeliers. "Men were not allowed in the dining room without jackets and women could not wear slacks. This kept up the dignity of the hotel," said Mrs. Harris.

"Men were not allowed in the dining room without jackets and women could not wear slacks. This kept up the dignity of the hotel."

Through their involvement with the Michigan Hotel Association, the Harris' became friends with Stewart Woodfill, owner of the Grand Hotel on Mackinac Island, and with Duncan Hines who presented the Whitcomb with a silver plaque reading "Twenty-five Years of Excellence in Food and Service."

The Whitcomb had 200 employees and 23 department heads. Among these were Eddie Mosimann who was their Swiss baker for 19 years, and Hans Kottmann who later owned the renowned Bit O'Swiss bakery in back of Tosi's Restaurant. Head chef was Fred Puhl, Eva Linderoth served as hostess for 28 years, Edna Sturgis waited tables for 33 years, and Crystal Thar was a waitress for 31 years.

The loyalty of the employees was mutually felt by the Harris'. Leon Harris called them his "Whitcomb Family." At an employee dinner in honor of his 50th birthday, Harris said, "The Whitcomb is the dearest place on earth for me." This feeling showed in the Whitcomb's commitment to excellence.

"You could help yourself to all the whipped cream you desired over the strawberry shortcake that you put together."

"Our Sunday smorgasbord was known far and wide. People would even drive from Chicago. We had huge bowls of shrimp. You could help yourself to all the real whipped cream you desired over the strawberry shortcake that you put together. Our Whitcomb Nut Cake, with its Bavarian cream filling, was a great specialty. During the week, planked white fish was in demand as well as our wonderful prime ribs of beef.

We had been at Lawry's in Los Angeles and saw them bake their roast beef in rock salt, so we did the same," said Mrs. Harris.

Many of St. Joseph's activities were held at the Whitcomb, including the 1934 centennial celebration. When World War II began, Mrs. Harris sold war bonds in the lobby. She became the only woman in the Midwest to sell more than one million dollars in bonds.

She became the only woman in the Midwest to sell more than one million dollars in war bonds.

Leon Harris passed away in 1964. At that time the hotel was leased to Zisook Hotel Systems until 1966. Soon after, it was sold to the Michigan Baptist Homes as a retirement center. Today, it is owned by the Vanguard Corporation. Its motto is, "...traditions we take special pride in: personal service, courteous attention, hospitality and good value." Just like the old days.

Chapter

Four

"Tell me a tale that dropped out of a star,
Push me a pun that is pungent, not earthy.
I must have something sharp, strident, and strong
To eke out a laugh or be moderately mirthy."

Verse from "Say When, and Say It"
by Ben King

A Sentimental Journey
to
Silver Beach Amusement Park

Silver Beach and its offspring, the Shadowland Ballroom, were made of memories and dreams. Today, there are sand dunes where calliope horses galloped in place, a roller coaster roared and Charleston dancers strutted their stuff.

"The whole idea was to have fun," said one St. Joseph resident who worked in the park. "Mr. Drake insisted on honesty from all of us, that's all, and we loved working there. He didn't want anyone cheated out of having a good time."

"The whole idea was to have fun."

Logan J. Drake's dreams for Silver Beach began in 1880 when, as an optimistic 17-year-old, he purchased some 20-22 acres of sand dunes from local Indians. He gave the Indians a year to move off the land. In the meantime, he started building.

His first love was boat building. Drawn to the water's edge, he had trouble deciding whether to purchase land on the St. Joseph River near the railroad tracks or to invest in the beach.

Drake started his boat construction and livery business which would build some 500 canoes and rowboats, sidepaddler steamers, and four launches.

He bought both parcels of property. The river property was purchased first from the Pere Marquette Railroad Company and was located west of the tracks. It was there that Drake started his boat construction and livery business which would build some 500 canoes and rowboats, sidepaddler steamers, and four launches.

Drake and Wallace Boat Livery located on the south side of the St. Joseph River east of the E. A. Graham dock.

River view of boat livery taken in August, 1896.

The Tourist *was built by her owner, L. J. Drake, and ran up the St. Joseph River to Buchanan and Berrien Springs in the early 1900s.*

59

The first launch was named *Wolverine* after Michigan's state animal, the second was *Buckeye*, the third *Tourist*, and the fourth, launched in 1915 and powered by a gasoline engine, was a 65-footer named *Milton D.*, after Drake's son. The launches were open on the sides like trolley cars and seated 60-100 people with benches on the sides and down the center. Powered first by steam and then by gasoline engines, the four launches cruised the St. Joseph River every hour on the hour from 1:00 P.M. to midnight for 50 cents round trip from about 1890 to 1924.

People would come by horse and buggy and spend all day on the riverboats which provided scenic tours from St. Joseph to Berrien Springs.

People would come by horse and buggy and spend all day on the riverboats which provided scenic tours from St. Joseph to Berrien Springs. In those days, there was no dam in Berrien Springs, so the tours reached Mott's Landing often

The Wolverine *launch built by L. J. Drake in approximately 1900-1910 ran up and down the river from St. Joseph to Berrien Springs.*

carrying capacity crowds. Box lunches and souvenirs made locally by Drake's restaurant and souvenir factory employees were available at the docks. The livery offered other motor boats for hire and small docks were built off the main dock for rowboats and canoes.

Drake teamed up with Louis D. Wallace in 1885. The men would later become brothers-in-law when they married the Schlenker sisters, Maude and Laura. In its first year of business, the firm of Drake and Wallace reported total profits of $6.50.

With the boat business running well, the partners turned their attention to the beach frontage with the intention of giving tourists more to do in St. Joseph. They formed the Silver Beach Amusement and Realty Company in 1891.

Drake and Wallace's first order of business was to remove the wigwams and shacks left by the Indians and to build ten cottages in their place. Eventually some 80 cottages would be available for vacationers to rent.

The first order of business was to remove wigwams and shacks left by the Indians and to build ten cottages in their place.

The resort enjoyed modest popularity, and Drake, then 28 years old, was proud of his investment. He and his bride-to-be, Maude Schlenker, spent part of their courtship walking on the beach. It was

Maude Schlenker coined the name Silver Beach because the moon path on the water "shimmered like silver."

she who coined the name *Silver Beach* because the moon path on the water "shimmered like silver." The couple married in 1902 and had three children.

In time, wooden concession stands were built with concessionaires invited to sell popular merchandise during the three to four month season. A water slide for children was anchored close to shore

The first cottages on the corner of Lake and Broad Streets. Eventually there were 80 cottages at Silver Beach.

Bath house, beach and water slides in August, 1896.

and Silver Beach was up and running. Photographs depict children in full bathing costumes—leggings, bloomers, water wings, shirts and hats—sitting at the top of the water slide as their parents watched from under umbrellas on shore.

Swimmers at Silver Beach on July 31, 1916.

The north end of Silver Beach circa 1916. L. J. Drake is the man on the left in the group of three men on the boardwalk. L. D. Wallace is in the vest standing alone. The Whitcomb, the moving stairway and a Graham and Morton coal burning ship are in the background.

Silver Beach grew in popularity along with the boating business. The Graham & Morton Transportation Company ran upper cabin propeller steamboats daily from St. Joseph to Chicago and Milwaukee. Two of these were named *Messenger* and *Sky Lark*. The crossing took about five hours—bringing thousands of tourists to St. Joseph and Benton Harbor—and enabled visitors to come for a day at the beach or stay the night in one of many nearby hotels.

A moving stairway was installed to carry people from the foot of the bluff at Vine Street to Lake Boulevard where some early hotels were located.

A moving stairway was installed to carry people from the foot of the bluff at Vine Street to Lake Boulevard where some early hotels were located and where the *Maids of the Mist* fountain at the Whitcomb Tower stands today. The stairway, popularly known as the "people mover," cost about a penny a ride, could go up or down and was run by Charlie Stevens.

During the next decade, Silver Beach expanded. Drake and company built an indoor swimming pool or natatorium in about 1900 or 1902. The bath house was 210 x 70 feet and 24 feet high, and was constructed for approximately $3,000. The pool used lake water which was heated by a steam furnace. Large skylights let sun in for additional heat and light. Lockers for women were upstairs, men's lockers were downstairs, and both

Reflections...the natatorium in 1921 was nicknamed "The Tank."

Old dance pavilion, circa 1916, was later made into the Fun House.

offered full bathing outfits and towels for rent.

In 1906, an indoor roller skating rink was built in a separate building north of the pool. Sometime during this period, a third building housing a dance pavilion or casino was also constructed. These activities and the penny arcade and concession stands drew huge crowds of tourists from Michigan as well as from Illinois and Wisconsin.

Drake and Wallace responded in about 1910 by adding a ride where dogs pulled children in carts around a turnstile, and in 1915 a merry-go-round and organ imported from Germany with hand-carved horses wearing jeweled saddles and real horse-hair tails, a House of Mysteries, and an airplane ride. The latter was installed in honor of a flight on Silver Beach in 1898—five years before Orville and Wilbur Wright flew at Kitty Hawk—when Augustus Moore Herring, a merchant and inventor in St. Joseph, was airborne in his homemade glider for an estimated 8-10 seconds over about 100 yards.

Augustus Moore Herring, a merchant and inventor in St. Joseph, was airborne in his homemade glider for an estimated 8-10 seconds over about 100 yards.

Later, Logan A. "Jack" Vilas became the first person to fly across Lake Michigan. He traveled from Silver Beach to Chicago in 1913. The 62-mile trip took about an hour and 40 minutes in an open cockpit bi-plane.

A new structure was built in 1917 to
house a bowling alley and 12 pool tables.
At the advent of the Roaring Twenties,
this became a quick success, but closed
in the thirties because indoor bowling
was too warm for summers in Michigan.

Silver Beach bowling alley in approximately 1920.

*Original pool tables and bowling alleys at Silver Beach in
approximately 1920.*

Silver Beach bowling alleys in approximately 1938.

Pool tables in Silver Beach bowling alleys in approximately 1938.

The dance pavilion by then was drawing top name musicians including Ted Weems and Wayne King the Waltz King, and medical students, Jules Stein, and brothers Billy and Eddie Goodhart. Stein, who played sax and clarinet, with Billy on piano and Eddie on bass horn, performed at the Silver Beach pavilion for five seasons with their twelve-piece orchestra.

The dance pavilion by then was drawing top name musicians including Ted Weems and Wayne King the Waltz King.

Seeing the success of the growing amusement park, Stein and Billy Goodhart talked to Drake about an idea they had. Drake encouraged the young medical students to "become the first and the best booking agents in the country." They went on to form the Music Corporation of America in the 1920s which would become the No. 1 booking

Jules Stein and Billy Goodhart went on to form the Music Corporation of America in the 1920s.

On the boardwalk at Silver Beach in 1921.

agent in the world. Drake himself brought in professional dancers to demonstrate the Charleston and local dancers were allowed to exhibit their skills on stage.

Views of the old wooden boardwalk in 1921-1922.

Silver Beach was reaching its peak. As its popularity grew, so did Drake's ideas. He replaced the original wooden boardwalk with a poured cement sidewalk which ran through the park's midway. In the 1920s, he added a roller coaster called *Chase Through the Clouds*

Silver Beach was reaching its peak. As its popularity grew, so did Drake's ideas.

At the bottom of the "Old Velvet" roller coaster.

71

which would become a symbol of the park, and an aeroplane ride. In 1925 an all male beauty contest was held to rival the women's annual bathing beauty contest which began in 1924.

Chase Through the Clouds *roller coaster was affectionately called "Old Velvet."*

Chase Through the Clouds *roller coaster in 1926.*

Aeroplane Ride.

Aeroplane Ride.

Also in 1925 Tuesdays became "Kiddies' Day" when children paid a discount price, about three cents a ride. Kiddies' Day became very popular with local families during the Great Depression of the thirties. They took picnic lunches with them and ate at tables in the roofed pavilion.

In May of 1927, with the dance pavilion going strong at the south end of the park, Drake opened Shadowland Ballroom at the opposite end near the channel. The new ballroom, a rotund wooden struc-

View of Silver Beach from Broad Street in 1928.

ture, was needed to hold the capacity crowds which the dance pavilion was drawing daily. Free carnations were given to the ladies on opening night.

Looking northeast over a crowded parking lot, circa 1928.

Shadowland Ballroom in progress in 1926-27. It opened in May, 1927.

Shadowland was elegantly decorated with 5,000 yards of silk pongee stretched between the arches and it had all indirect lighting. In the late thirties, it was redecorated in a modern style.

Shadowland Ballroom in 1927.

Shadowland Ballroom was redecorated to this Art Deco style in 1938-39.

As the big band era came into fashion, Shadowland Ballroom drew musicians such as Lawrence Welk, Kay Kyser, Oliver Naylor, George Olsen, Jan Garber, Woody Herman and Victor Young. Dances were held seven nights a week with Sunday matinees.

Jim Miller of Benton Harbor remembers some of the local bands who played there. He sometimes sat in on drums with groups led by Del Pino and Bob Lewis.

"It didn't cost anything to get into Shadowland other than on big band nights," Miller recalls. "Dance tickets were ten cents each or three for a quarter, eight for 50 cents, 20 for a dollar. A coke and a bag of chips were a nickel each. We danced to such romantic tunes as *Red Sails in the Sunset, Slow Boat to China, Hands Across the Table, Stars Fell on Alabama* and *Cocktails for Two*."

"Dance tickets were ten cents each or three for a quarter, eight for 50 cents, 20 for a dollar. A coke and a bag of chips were a nickel each."

The old dance pavilion was converted to a Fun House, complete with a spinning saucer, distorted mirrors, revolving barrel, sugar bowl, and a two-lane, handmade, maple slide said to be the tallest in the state at the time it was built.

The old dance pavilion was converted to a Fun House.

Next to the Fun House a Mirror Maze was installed with mirrors to confuse the person inside whose object was to get to the back for a look at distorted mirrors and then get outside again.

Sugar Bowl ride in the Fun House.

Fun House slide built in 1927.

Drake's philosophy was to change the park to keep the amusements interesting and up-to-date. He supervised much of the construction himself with his knowledge of boat building and was able to make the renovations less costly.

Drake's philosophy was to change the park to keep the amusements interesting and up-to-date.

Many celebrities came to Silver Beach over the years. Actors Joe E. Brown and Ben Blue, both of Benton Harbor, fighters Jack Dempsey and Joe Louis, actresses Lana Turner, Ava Gardner, Janet Gaynor and Jean Harlow were among the visitors.

In the depression of the 1930s, Shadowland Ballroom stayed open 24 hours for marathon dances when couples competed for cash prizes and big crowds of spectators cheered on the sidelines. One *Herald-Press* story from 1930 said that the Michigan State Department of Labor tried "to halt the fallen-arch derby." But a postponement was obtained allowing the weary dancers to finish.

In the depression of the 1930s, Shadowland Ballroom stayed open 24 hours for marathon dances.

Tourists continued to ride the Graham & Morton and other boat lines which helped Silver Beach survive the Great Depression. During this time, the Grigsby-Grunow Company of Chicago brought 2,000 of its employees to Silver Beach for a Friday outing. They were transported by *The Alabama* and *The*

City of Holland, two Goodrich Transportation steamers.

Drake added a ride called The Whip *and 12-14 electric bumper cars called* The Scooter.

In the early 1930s, Drake added a ride called *The Whip* and 12-14 electric bumper cars called *The Scooter* which were located in a new building with a steel floor. Bertha Hopp was employed as a cashier for many years. She would hold a couple's baby so they could enjoy a fast ride.

The Whip *with Shadowland Ballroom in the background.*

In the mid-thirties, a speedboat was introduced to the public for fast rides on the river and the lake. At about the same time, wrestling matches became popular and a ring was set up behind the roller coaster.

Wallace sold his share of the park to Drake in the late 1930s, and Drake began to rely on his son-in-law, H. J. "Chief" Terrill, for assistance with the park. Terrill brought fresh ideas to Silver Beach including a boat landing for tourists who wanted to stop directly at the park instead of going farther down river to the main docks where shuttle buses waited to entice people to other places.

Terrill brought fresh ideas to Silver Beach including a boat landing for tourists.

The Scooter *at Silver Beach in 1954.*

The swimming pool closed in the 1940s, and the thriving penny arcade was expanded in its place.

The swimming pool closed in the 1940s, and the thriving penny arcade was expanded in its place. The arcade was renamed Play Drome Arcade and featured pinball and candy machines, rifle shooting, miniature bowling and a postcard machine. The roller rink was replaced with a *Pretzel* ride and a haunted house ride called *Laff in the Dark*. A rodeo was brought in, a strawberry festival was held in June and fireworks went off in July. A ferris wheel and a miniature train were built around 1945.

During World War II, dancing at Shadowland slowed down a bit, but was fondly remembered by Betty (Gast)

Gaunder of St. Joseph as "the place to be." She sang with the Bob Lewis band for about a year and a half, and met her husband, George—who was a lifeguard at Silver Beach for several years—at Shadowland.

"Girls in pleated skirts and saddle shoes and servicemen in uniform were a part of the scene," she recalls. "Gas rationing was in effect so we shared the ride and came by the carload. We danced to *Woodchopper's Ball, Strictly Instrumental* and *One O'Clock Jump.* I remember well the more sentimental wartime songs like *I'll Walk Alone, I'll Be Seeing You, I'll be Home for Christmas* as well as *Goodnight Sweetheart,* the song which concluded each evenings dancing."

Girls in pleated skirts and saddle shoes and servicemen in uniform were a part of the scene.

On July 5, 1945, Louis Wallace died at the age of 80; and on September 27, 1947, Logan Drake passed away at the age of 83 leaving the Silver Beach Amusement and Realty Company to his widow and to his daughter who had become the wife of H. J. "Chief" Terrill. Terrill was named president of the company. Mrs. Drake passed away in 1965.

The Terrills continued to change the amusements to attract tourists. Kiddieland, a feature in the 1950s, had a boat ride, an airplane ride, a minia-

The Terrills continued to change the amusements to attract tourists.

ture merry-go-round and a miniature train for smaller children. A miniature golf course was added in 1951.

Lee Sies built the *River Queen* excursion boat in 1955. A 65-foot stern-wheeled riverboat, Sies operated it up the river from Silver Beach for ten years on the St. Joseph River and for five years in Grand Haven.

By the sixties, Silver Beach was beginning to show its age...

By the sixties, Silver Beach was beginning to show its age, despite efforts to paint and repair the park every spring. But the Terrills carried on introducing go-karts, a *Swingin' Gym*, a *Rock-O-Plane*, *Tarantula*, the *Tilt-A-Whirl* and many more rides some of which opened for only one or two seasons.

Michigan winters contributed to the park's constant need for repairs. Heavy snows caused abut 10 feet of the flat midway roof near the north end to collapse in 1967.

The crime rate rose in the park as bus loads of tourists replaced the more genteel visitors who had formerly arrived on steamships. Pick-pockets, purse-snatching, fights and general rowdiness caused the park to close on August 10, 1970. At the end of that season, the park went up for sale.

St. Joseph's chief safety inspector, Carl Conklin, estimated that $50,000 in electrical wiring and plumbing improvements were needed. In the ensuing years, rides and equipment were sold. Finally, the roller coaster was dismantled in 1974.

Silver Beach Amusement Park, an attraction in St. Joseph since 1891, stood empty until 1975 when it was demolished in a controlled fire on October 2.

LECO Corporation of St. Joseph purchased the property on November 22, 1977. Silver Beach was used as a city beach until the late 1980s when it was leased to the Berrien County Parks for one dollar for continued use as a public beach.

The Silver Beach Amusement Park, an attraction in St. Joseph since 1891, stood empty until 1975 when it was demolished.

Chapter

Five

"I know her by all that is good, kind and true,
This modest young maiden I name;
I've walked with her, talked with her,
Danced with her, too,
And found that my heart was aflame;
I've written her letters, and small billet-doux,
Revealing my love in each line;
You can drink to your slim, satin-bodiced gazelle,
But the girl with the jersey is mine."

Verse from "The Girl with the Jersey"
by Ben King

The YWCA
of
Southwestern Michigan
(Young Women's Christian Association)

Kate Cartter felt that there was little wholesome entertainment for women in St. Joseph around the turn of the Twentieth Century. When she decided to do something about it, the nucleus for the YWCA of Southwestern Michigan was formed to provide recreation for young women who worked.

...the nucleus for the YWCA of Southwestern Michigan was formed to provide recreation for working women.

Cartter first organized a reading class in 1908 which met in private homes. Many of the members were recruited from Cooper, Wells & Co. which was the city's largest industrial plant. As a former Cooper, Wells & Co. cmployee, Cartter knew there were about 600 working women at the factory. Others were employed elsewhere downtown.

Members of the Reading Class, 1908
Anna Finnegan, Ida Eckert, Helen Clarke, Belle Miller, Mary Beauman, Grace Sullivan, Frances Hull, Elva Wheeler, Susie & Sophia Gobiel, Mable Schnerder, Lillia Sprague, Olive Freitag, Rae Blackman, Frances Wilson, Norma Schivendener, Nellie Benning, Bertha Jackson, Sophia Stanton, Mrs. R. B. Creheve, Mrs. E. J. Witt, Mrs. T. G. Dickinson, Mrs. W. J. Cleary, Mrs. C. W. Danforth.

Cartter was soon joined by Mrs. A. H. Stoneman and Catherine Sullivan in her pursuit to organize activities for women. Together they rented second floor rooms for $10 a month in the Wells Block above the G. C. Murphy Company at 307 State Street to continue the reading group and meet for lunch.

The women prepared the food in their homes and carried steaming kettles upstairs to the dingy back rooms.

The "working girls," as they were referred to then, brought their lunches and enjoyed the companionship. To raise money for the group, Stoneman and Sullivan decided to supplement the box lunches with hot coffee, potatoes, bread and butter. The two women prepared the food in their homes and carried steaming kettles up the stairs to the dingy back rooms.

Stoneman wrote, "the first (hot) meal was served in that forlorn room in the Wells Block and we all stared out the window at the blank wall of the Rimes and Hildebrand store. There were no lights or stove and the stairs were filthy." That day's profits amounted to eleven cents.

To take financial pressure off the group, Stoneman and Sullivan assumed the rent payment. The women continued to meet for reading and lunch. They added evening exercises to their program with Stoneman acting as instructor.

During this time the women investigated YWCA requirements. Several group members knew what YWCAs had done in other cities, and they wanted to offer similar services in St. Joseph. National requirements for a YWCA charter included membership comprised of 200 women.

With the help of Mrs. Arthur Moffat, Stoneman and Sullivan organized 57 women into a club. They begged money from every possible source in the twin cities and purchased some Indian clubs and dumbbells for the exercise classes.

Mrs. W. F. Morley, a former physical education director at the YWCA in Minneapolis, became one of the group's most inspiring leaders. According to Stoneman, "the door opened one evening and a radiantly beautiful girl stood there and just said, 'May I be of any help to you?'"

"The door opened one evening and a radiantly beautiful girl stood there and just said, 'May I be of any help to you?'"

On May 29, 1909 the St. Joseph Girls Club became a YWCA with Stoneman serving as president. Charter executive board members were: Stoneman, Mrs. H. S. Whitney, Mrs. J. H. Graham, Kate Cartter, Mrs. C. L. Marquardt, Mrs. T. G. Dickinson, Mrs. C. M. Sullivan, Frances Hull, Mrs. B. F. McConnell, Mrs. A. B. Moffat, Madeline McConnell, Dr. Hattie Schwendener, Mrs. W. F.

Morley, Anne Finnegan, Elizabeth Hooper and Helen Clark.

Dr. Hattie Schwendener, a charter executive board member of the YWCA.

Upon recommendation of the National YWCA, the local board hired a full-time secretary, Hettie Anderson. Stoneman wrote that "I met her (Anderson) at the train quaking in my boots because we had to pay her sixty dollars a month, and we hadn't an idea in the world where it was to come from. But Hettie just said 'If I can't earn my own salary by the time I've been here a month, I'll go home where I belong.'" In her first month Anderson raised $200.

About Anderson, Stoneman wrote, "She had a Midas touch for raising money and an outstanding spiritual attitude toward life...she just used to talk to people in a pleasant way and there you were. The money would just roll in...she seemed to gather in money without even moving from a chair."

"She had a Midas touch for raising money and an outstanding spiritual attitude toward life."

Within a year, the new YWCA had moved to Mrs. T. T. Ransom's house on the corner of Lake Boulevard at Elm Street where cafeteria style lunches were served. Gym classes were held in Maccabees Hall on the second floor of what is now Troost Brother's Furniture on the corner of State and Broad Streets. Excursions, picnics and lawn parties were organized and educational classes were taught on demand by Sullivan and Moffat.

Six meal tickets sold for one dollar.

Lunches were served in the cafeteria from 11:30 a.m. to 1:00 p.m. with six meal tickets selling for one dollar. YWCA organizers cooked the food so that all profits could go to the general fund. Stoneman's brown bread was popular and she baked as many as ten loaves a day for sale in the cafeteria.

Anderson began vesper services at the Ransom house and moved the cafeteria to the Kingsley house at 413 State Street. In time, all YWCA functions were also moved to the Kingsley house except for the gym classes which continued at Maccabees Hall.

While they were striving toward national YWCA affiliation, the group achieved a different yet important goal of cooperation between Benton Harbor and St. Joseph.

In 1910, 170 women signed a charter organizing the group into an official twin city association. While they were striving toward national YWCA affiliation, the group achieved a different yet important goal of cooperation between the cities of Benton Harbor and St. Joseph. It was their hope to improve quality of life in the communities by increasing the well-being of women.

By national standards, it was unprecedented to form a YWCA without the required 200 members. As the local group moved toward affiliation, they drew up their petition for incorporation and listed the financial assets of the cafeteria. They were the only YWCA in

94

the country to operate a paying cafeteria.

"Of course," Stoneman said, "after I had finished paying the first month's bills for the association, I only had seven cents left in my pocket. It would have been a catastrophe if the national headquarters had asked to see our bank balance."

The women realized their goal on April 5, 1911 when the group became a part of the national YWCA and St. Joseph became the smallest city in Michigan to have a YWCA. That summer, members installed an information booth at 817 Broad Street to aid visitors coming to St. Joseph by train or boat. Mrs. J. E. Beers volunteered to meet every boat and train—even the 3:00 a.m. boat— with information about where to eat and sleep and find entertainment.

Mrs. Beers met every boat and train, even the 3:00 a.m. boat, with information about where to eat and sleep and find entertainment.

Beers had a list of all stores, restaurants and boarding houses within walking distance of the downtown. The house at 1446 Lake Boulevard, called The Esnor, accommodated 30 people and quoted rates of $8 to $10 per week for room and board.

Also in 1911, YWCA members entered into "a long fight with the city council" for the erection of lights along the bluff.

YWCA members entered into "a long fight with the city council" for the erection of lights along the bluff.

*With many trav-
elers coming to St.
Joseph, young
women were apt to
be "waylaid by
wandering young
men" along the
lake bluff.*

With many travelers coming to St. Joseph, young women were apt to be "waylaid by wandering young men" along the lake bluff. Their two-year fight was successful in 1913 when "a vigilante committee descended upon Mayor Wallace and his cohorts at a city council meeting and demanded action on their petition."

Anderson left the YWCA and was succeeded in her position as general secretary by Louise Lindauer. Frances Hull became director, and Mrs. Lou Smith was matron of association rooms. The

Room at 413 State Street October, 1912.

board held their second annual banquet and reported that 11,162 persons had been served in the cafeteria during 1911. A lunch of hot soup or coffee with bread and butter cost ten cents.

As the organization grew, members held social events, continued their work in the cafeteria, ran the Traveller's (sic) Aid information booth, held exercise classes and other activities. A musical club was formed called the Do-Drop-In.

In 1912, the YWCA sponsored a production of *Pygmalian and Galatea*, continued vesper services, sponsored several visiting lecturers and musicians, held Bible discussions and classes in French, German, "correct English," cooking, embroidery and tatting. Gym classes were still held in Maccabees Hall while other activities took place in YWCA rooms at 413 State Street.

With Stoneman still serving as president, the third annual meeting was held on May 26, 1912. It was reported that two clubs for younger girls had been organized: the Comrade Club for ages 9 to 14 offered sewing, games and stories; and the T.M.T.M. (The More The Merrier) club for ages 14 to 18 featured sewing and gymnastics.

More than 11,000 persons had been served in the cafeteria in 1911. A lunch of hot soup or coffee with bread and butter cost ten cents.

*She reported as-
sisting more than
1,000 persons
that year with
special attention
to 50 cases in-
cluding a 16-
year-old girl
"from the Chicago
boat who was
fleeing from a
young man who
seemed interested
in her for no good
reason."*

Ruth Hanna was introduced as the new
general secretary, Eva Hardin became
physical director, and Beers was again
chosen to run the Traveller's Aid. The
following year, Beers' job became a paid
position. She reported assisting more
than 1,000 persons that year with special attention to 50 cases including a 16-
year-old girl "from the Chicago boat who
was fleeing from a young man who
seemed interested in her for no good
reason."

Also in 1913, the group held a circus on
Main Street in addition to their regular
program of activities. The cafeteria was
overhauled to allow more space for serving meals and the first Christmas open
house was held. Mrs. William Cleary
became president for 1913-14.

When the association moved to the second floor of the 505 Building on the
corner of Pleasant Street and Lake Boulevard in 1914, it was the first time all of
the YWCA functions were gathered under one roof. Progress was exciting, but
had its ups and downs.

*The stairway had
no railing until
Stoneman fell
down the stairs
one icy day and
was caught by
Lloyd Clark who
promptly ob-
tained a railing
for the building.*

There was no inside stairway, so members used an iron stairway attached to
the outside of the building. The stairway had no railing until Stoneman fell
down the stairs one icy day and was
caught by Lloyd Clark. Clark promptly
obtained a railing for the building.

Portrait of an early YWCA Board of Directors.

View of the rest room February, 1915.

*Some board members on
February 10, 1915.*

General secretary at her desk on February 26, 1915.

Nellie Benning served as cafeteria director in 1914 turning a profit of $11,000 that year. As the cafeteria grew, board members donated furniture for the dining room and "quaked during the first month after they ordered a $200 steam table for the counter. But at the end of six weeks it had been paid for and another one ordered."

The board found that a private dining room for family and club parties and business luncheons was a financial success. The women still cooked much of the food in their own homes and brought it to the cafeteria each day.

The board found that a private dining room for family and club parties and business luncheons was a financial success.

In the excitement of 1914, an open house was held and the year's program included children's gym classes, business English, first aid and basket weaving in addition to regular classes. Three more clubs for young girls were formed.

The following years saw the YWCA concentrate on fund raising, membership, entertainment, physical education, a variety of classes and social concerns. In 1915 the association rooms "were proudly decorated with a six by eight metal sign saying *YWCA CAFETERIA AND REST ROOMS*." By the end of that year, the YWCA had 300 members.

*They became in-
volved in food
conservation, ar-
ranged for "host-
ess houses" to
comfort the fami-
lies of service-
men, and con-
ducted a survey
of community so-
cial concerns.*

In 1917 and 1918 the group assisted the World War I effort working with the YMCA to provide rest huts for service-men overseas. They became involved in food conservation, arranged for "hostess houses" to comfort the families of ser-vicemen, and conducted a survey of com-munity social concerns. They focused on international events and hosted speak-ers from other countries.

A new lunch program was initiated in 1919 for employed women. Long tables were installed in the gymnasium for seating in addition to that in the cafete-ria. Lunchtime included games and dancing directed by the gym instructor.

*During Witt's
term as presi-
dent, the YWCA
increased its in-
ternational out-
look by hosting
foreign speakers.*

Marjorie Upton and Mrs. Paul Witt served as advisors for a national mili-tary organization for girls aged 12 to 18 called the Girl Reserves (this group would later become the Y-Teens). Mrs. E. J. Witt served as YWCA president from 1916 to 1921. During her term, the as-sociation increased its international outlook by hosting foreign speakers.

More Girl Reserves Corps were formed, a dramatics class was held, and a club called the Sunshine Sisters was started by Ruth Irwin. That club hosted a sum-mer camp for girls at Camp Gray near Riverside in response to the national association's drive for more girls' recreation. In the fall of 1919 fund raisers were held to benefit child welfare work and the United Charities. Another club was formed for students. According to the *Herald-Press*, men were invited to a party at the YWCA when "the board decided to open the doors to gentlemen friends of the girls."

Men were invited to a party at the YWCA when "the board decided to open the doors to gentlemen friends of the girls."

The association became known officially as the Benton Harbor-St. Joseph YWCA in 1920 to draw more women into membership. That year a constitution was adopted to expand services throughout Berrien County . Employed women at Auto Specialties and Cooper, Wells & Co. formed respective clubs, and girls clubs were started for Benton Harbor students.

The association continued its interest in physical education with the formation of the Twin City Industrial Athletic Association whose members bowled at the Pfeister Alleys in Benton Harbor. Rotary wives, church groups and small business girls' clubs met in YWCA rooms, and more new clubs were formed under the YW umbrella.

In 1921 membership was 577 with a budget of $32,393. In addition, the group received a generous anonymous donation. This came at an opportune time since the association had an option to

In 1921 membership was 577 with a budget of $32,393. In addition, the group received a generous anonymous donation.

The lot was purchased by the YWCA on March 30, 1921 for $16,000.

buy property known as the Murphy and Morrison corner at Lake Boulevard and Pleasant Street. This lot was purchased by the YWCA on March 30, 1921 for $16,000.

According to Mrs. Stoneman, this was made possible "due to the open-heartedness of Mr. T. G. Dickinson whose wife had long been a 'fairy god-mother' to the association." He had formerly wished to repay Stoneman for her work with a personal gift, but she insisted upon a gift to the YW instead. When Stoneman heard about the anonymous donor, she "knew that Dickinson had not forgotten that conversation." At the time of purchase the Imperial Lunchroom and a residence were demolished. YWCA members built a temporary skating rink on the site.

He had wished to repay Stoneman for her work with a personal gift, but she insisted upon a gift to the YW instead.

One of the women's groups formed by the YWCA was the Progress Club. It became a member of the Michigan Business and Professional Women's Association. Other groups were organized including a book club, sewing class, Twin City Storytellers' League, Kiwanis Club, "Y" Girls, Pocomoke Club.

A new constitution was adopted in 1921 and the name changed to the Berrien County YWCA.

A new constitution was adopted in 1921 and the association changed its name to the Berrien County YWCA. As such, members participated in dedication ceremonies for the new Methodist Peace Temple in Benton Harbor, promoted "three days of educational advancement and general well-being in the community," and sponsored the Mutual Lyceum Chautauqua. Since 1909 the staff had grown from one to three secretaries and a cafeteria manager.

The building committee planned four public meetings in 1922. The land purchase was completed and the deed was recorded in the Berrien County clerk's office. Building committee members were George Pixley, E. C. Campbell, Mrs. Vincent Switzer, Mrs. W. L. Wilson and Arthur G. Preston.

Building committee members were George Pixley, E. C. Campbell, Mrs. Vincent Switzer, Mrs. W. L. Wilson and Arthur G. Preston.

A campaign committee to fund the building was also organized. Its members were Louis Upton, chairman, F. J. Bradford, Ray W. Davis, J. O. Wells, Mrs. W. L. Wilson, Frank Jensen, W. A. Vawter.

YWCA clubs remained active, and new ones were formed. These were the M. M. Club for Girls, a married women's group for basketball and bowling, and the St. Joseph City Federation of Women's Clubs whose primary purpose was to establish a public comfort station in the city.

Building plans progressed through 1923. On January 19, 1924 the YWCA received a pledge of $15,000 from philanthropist Mrs. Henrietta Avery of Benton Harbor on condition that the association would raise an additional $85,000 and would begin construction by January 1, 1925. A capital fund drive began January 30, 1924 which raised $92,000 in the first three days.

Headquarters for the building fund were set up in the Whitcomb Hotel. Major B. M. Clerk was campaign director, Fred Tebbe was head of the building committee, and G. DeWitt Robinson chaired the soliciting teams. When a swimming pool was added to building plans, the fund goal jumped from $150,000 to $175,000, but was soon cut back to $150,000 with the elimination of items deemed unessential. Arthur Preston became the new campaign chairman. Robert Lager of Chicago was selected as architect.

On the national scene, YWCA headquarters announced that voting privileges would extend to all members. They stated that "race and creed must not matter in the conduct of YWCA affairs."

The building committee held their ground breaking ceremonies on December 20, 1924 in compliance with Mrs. Avery's terms. The contract was let to the Max Stock Construction Company.

This commercial building on the east side of Lake Boulevard between Pleasant and Broad Streets stands on the site of the YWCA.

Groundbreaking ceremonies for the YWCA building shows Mrs. W. J. Cleary of Benton Harbor turning the first shovel full of earth.

The building was completed on December 31, 1925.

While fund raising for the structure continued, the cornerstone for the YWCA building at 508 Pleasant Street was laid during ceremonies on June 24, 1925. The committee honored past presidents Stoneman, McConnell, Cleary, Witt, Vawter and Longenecker. Copies of the *Herald-Press*, coins and YWCA mementoes were sealed inside the cornerstone. The building was completed on December 31, 1925.

With the new building, membership drives escalated and fund raising continued. The association celebrated with five days of dedication ceremonies followed by a number of open house events. Programming expanded with emphasis on world fellowship, education, recreation, exercise and youth.

The annual membership campaigns and fund drives were successful for the YWCA throughout the early 1900s. It was a time for growth in programming and personnel for the group. Strong leadership swelled from the community to work in the YWCA, and the association prospered.

In the early 1930s a business recession was felt locally and the YWCA responded with creative programming on a decreased budget. In 1932, 30 men and women met at the Louis Upton home in Edgewater to organize the Twin City Theater Guild (now Twin City Players). The guild presented plays and held their meetings for several years at the YWCA.

The depression was fully felt by 1933, and YWCA President Frances Laity said, "The banks have failed, but the dividends in community service through the twin city YWCA still continue." Registration for classes reached an all-time high in 1933, and went up again in 1934.

"The banks have failed, but the dividends in community service through the twin city YWCA still continue."

The pool closed in 1934 for financial reasons, but recreational and educational activities continued. The Theater Guild changed their name to Twin City Players and produced an adaptation of *The Wizard of Oz.*

The YWCA set up an employment service which placed 375 women out of the 650 who sought work.

With mass unemployment in the area, the YWCA set up an employment service which placed 375 women out of the 650 who sought work.

Records state that the community was "counting heavily on the YW to provide inexpensive, entertaining recreation. The Twin City Players cheered everyone up in the fall with their exciting presentation of the melodrama *Gold in the Hills.*"

The building debt was paid off in 1936, but the pool remained closed. Social and athletic events, along with plays, classes and meetings were well attended. Groups and recreational offerings continued to evolve and change.

In 1937 the YWCA received an anonymous New Year's gift of $1,000 to reopen the pool.

The YWCA received an anonymous New Year's gift of $1,000 in 1937 to reopen the pool. With the money in hand, a YWCA committee urged the city commission to furnish free water for the pool for a four month period. The pool was reopened on January 20, 1937. That year's budget included money for pool maintenance and the fall fund drive raised $10,700 for the pool and building repairs.

An attempt was made during 1937 to organize fund raising into a community chest to benefit service agencies including the hospital, scouts, Salvation Army, YWCA and YMCA. But according to John Stubblefield, who had been appointed chairman of the project, "the public was not enough interested in unifying all annual civic and philanthropic drives."

Area churches met at the YWCA to discuss the coalition of county churches into a council, a nutritional institute was held by public health nurses, and the first Cotillion Dance was given for young people by their parents.

In 1938, J. N. Klock died. He had long been a benefactor of the YWCA and was the organizer of the first Twin City Coordinating Council. Local focus that year was on youth programs. With the aim to provide guidance and recreation for youth, representatives from several community groups planned summer youth programs. A youth hostel, originally opened in 1936 in Benton Harbor, was reopened.

The years between 1940 and 1975 saw the formation of several lasting community groups. Among these were a new chapter of the American Association of University Women (1941), the Twin City Community Chest—now called the Blossomland United Way—(1942), and a great books discussion group (1947).

Girl Reserves changed its name to Y-Teens (1945), and The Link grew from YWCA concern for runaway teenagers (1973).

The YWCA offered citizenship classes enabling new citizens to receive their first United States papers, sponsored water safety courses and held art exhibits. The group was selected out of 1,476 associations in the country by the foreign division of the national organization in 1940 as the location for a visiting secretary to study YWCA methods here. In 1942 the building was redecorated and in 1945 the cafeteria closed with the resulting space dedicated to a "Cove" for young people.

As the first YWCA formed in a small city, the local association existed in the 1950s as a hub of community leadership. Its purpose was "To build fellowship of women and girls devoted to the task of realizing in our common life those ideals of personal and social living to which we are committed by our faith as Christians. In this endeavor we seek to understand Jesus, to share His love for all people, and to grow in the knowledge and love of God."

In 1955 the YWCA purchased the Lake View Hotel property at 309 Lake Boulevard for $33,000. A building addition

In 1955 the YWCA purchased the Lake View Hotel property at 309 Lake Boulevard for $33,000.

was constructed in 1958 which included a new kitchen, a community room and fireside lounge. By 1959 the membership totaled 3,255.

The association changed its name to the YWCA of Southwestern Michigan during the 1980s. This was a period of hard times for the group. With YWCA personnel and volunteers struggling to survive, the building was closed in November, 1987 for major repairs including replacing the boiler, installing smoke detectors, sprinklers and fire doors. The swimming pool and deck were regrouted, handrails were repaired, and an automatic chemical feeder and heater were added. Additional electrical, plumbing and structural repairs were made to bring the building up to code. Most of the programs were temporarily terminated during the eight months that the building was closed and the future of the YWCA seemed in jeopardy.

With YWCA personnel and volunteers struggling to survive, the building was closed in November, 1987 for major repairs.

When the building reopened on July 5, 1988, YW membership was only 454. Programming resumed in the newly redecorated facility with a concentration on exercise in the pool and in the gym. By 1989, membership had increased to more than 1,400.

By 1989, membership had increased to more than 1,400.

Also in 1989, a capital fund drive began to raise $775,000 for the building fund, the endowment fund, and for programming. By 1990, some $585,000 had been pledged to support the YWCA. Plans were made to bring full-time day care and a preschool to the YWCA, and building renovations continued.

"...collective power toward elimination of racism wherever it exists and by any means necessary."

The YWCA purpose has evolved to include a worldwide membership movement for women of all ages. Its purpose now reflects the YWCA's overriding priority which is "collective power toward the elimination of racism wherever it exists and by any means necessary."

The YWCA of Southwestern Michigan in 1988.

YWCA PURPOSE

The Young Women's Christian Association of the United States of America, a movement rooted in the Christian faith as known in Jesus and nourished by the resources of that faith, seeks to respond to the barrier-breaking love of God in this day.

The Association draws together into responsible membership women and girls of diverse experiences and faiths, that their lives may be open to new understanding and deeper relationships and that together they may join in the struggle for peace and justice, freedom and dignity for all people.

Chapter

Six

"I don't p'tend to write, an' ain't
One of them 'air chaps 't paint;
'F I was I'd tell of scenes 't lie
Stretched out afore a feller's eye;
Er when the sun was hangin' low
I'd paint it right from Old St. Joe."

Verse from "Old St. Joe"
by Ben King

St. Joseph Art Association
and
Krasl Art Center

The St. Joseph Art Association owns 17,000 square feet of space at the Krasl Art Center. One of its activities is a juried summer Art Fair that attracts 70,000 people during the two day annual event. The association also boasts loyalty from hundreds of volunteers.

Phyllis Rhoads was president for the first two years of the association, which from its inception in 1962 was devoted to giving artists within a 50-mile radius of St. Joseph an opportunity to exhibit and sell their work. "I remember sitting in the backyard of our house with a group of my students and some others," said Rhoads. "We talked about what could be done for our art. When I came here in 1949 nothing was going on in art. It was sad. I had come from Cleveland and knew what could be done."

"We talked about what could be done for our art. When I came here in 1949 nothing was going on in art. It was sad."

She began by teaching portrait and figure drawing in her home on Lake Boulevard and talking about art to her stu-

Heading a group of artists sounds like trying to stuff toothpaste back into a tube.

dents and friends. Being the head of a group of artists sounds like trying to stuff toothpaste back into a tube, but Rhoads says, "We never felt like volunteer workers. We wanted to do something with art."

In addition to Rhoads, the original art fair committee included Francis Bradford, John Duymovic, Roy Gross, Madelyn Haas, Carol Howard, Eric Johnson, Emily Parks Cooper, Dorothy Schwerdt, Alice Van Scyoc, Foster Willey and Dorothy Witkoske. As a result of meetings with these artists, students and business people, the St. Joseph Art Association was eventually formed.

The first "Arts and Crafts Fair" took place on a quiet July day in 1962 at Lake Bluff Park. It attracted a crowd of about 3,000 to 5,000 people and nearly 100 artists from southwestern Michigan and northern Indiana.

"The first shows were hung on clothes lines. If the work got a little heavy, the lines hung down, but people came to see."

The second outdoor fair, held in 1963, had to be postponed due to rain and high winds, but despite the delay, its crowd doubled in size to an estimated 10,000 visitors. Phyllis Rhoads acted as chairperson for both fairs. "The first shows were hung on clothes lines. If the work got a little heavy, the lines hung down, but people came to see. People came," she said.

Carol Ladrow joined the group in 1963. She was asked by Cay Beckmann to help bring the Detroit Institute of Art's traveling "Artmobile" to the fair, which she accomplished in 1964. That year, the exhibitors drew an estimated 15,000 spectators. "The fair was the big thing for years," says Ladrow. "We didn't have two quarters to rub together, and everything was done by volunteers. We all did every job at one time or another."

"We didn't have two quarters to rub together, and everything was done by volunteers."

The art fair committee officially organized into the St. Joseph Art Association (SJAA) in 1964. A constitution was written with a goal of promoting interest in the arts through exhibits and education. Phyllis Rhoads acted as advisor to elected officers: Roy Gross, president; Alice Van Scyoc, vice president; Emily Parks Cooper, secretary; and John Duymovic, treasurer.

They met regularly in space provided by the YWCA, located at 508 Pleasant Street, on the corner of Lake Boulevard across the street from the site of the art fair. By 1965, the art fair crowd was approximately 20,000, with 125 artists participating. Cay Beckmann was president that year. She remembers the meetings in Rhoads' backyard, and the enthusiasm of the early years. "It was all very basic," Beckmann said. "The first art fair program was a sheet with

50 names. The committee worked on it, and the community was ready for it. It clicked. We were at the right place at the right time and it worked. From that, others became involved. I think it was well accepted because it was needed."

In 1966, Phyllis Rhoads again took the helm of the association, with Dorothy Schwerdt as co-president.

"...To promote, develop and encourage the showing and study of paintings, sculptures, graphic reproductions, and fine arts of significant artistic, literary and educational value."

The SJAA was incorporated as a non-profit organization in 1967. Its purpose was, in part, "To promote, develop and encourage the showing and study of paintings, sculptures, graphic reproductions, and fine arts of significant artistic, literary and educational value."

Don and Edie Walton served as co-presidents in 1967 and 1968. They helped to coordinate the association's first membership drive. As a non-profit organization, the group was now able to collect and use funds to achieve their goals. They were making money on the art fair and on memberships.

SJAA members gave another fund raising event in 1968. This was a tour of residences with significant art collections. The tour included the homes of George and Olga Krasl, Juel Ranum, Dr. and Mrs. Dean Ray, M. S. "Dusty" and Phyllis Rhoads, and Mr. and Mrs. H. Stewart Ross.

Also in 1968 the association made plans to use Memorial Hall as an art center. Under that proposal the veterans hall, 415 Lake Boulevard, located one block south of the YWCA, was to be refurbished to hold art classes, meetings and lectures as well as provide gallery space. The veterans would use the basement as their meeting place.

However, as the St. Joseph City Commission worked on a lease for the SJAA, several veterans groups marched on City Hall in protest at being restricted to the basement. The veterans won this fight, preventing the SJAA from converting the hall.

The SJAA continued meeting monthly in the YWCA. By 1969, in its eighth year, the art fair had grown to 116 exhibitors and drew an estimated 25,000 people to St. Joseph.

By 1969, in its eighth year, the fair had grown to 116 exhibitors and drew an estimated 25,000 people to St. Joseph.

In 1970 and 1971 Cay Beckmann was reappointed president. Meetings were still held in the YWCA, but two series of classes were held at Memorial Hall. These were organized and presented by artists/teachers Dorothy Miller, Jean Battles, Phyllis Rhoads and Barbara Jaeger. Growing and active, the SJAA was in need of a place of its own.

In 1970 Candace Seymour won the SJAA's first Christmas card contest for high school students, and Foster Willey, Jr. won the next year's contest. The St. Joseph High School Art Club's $100 donation to the SJAA in 1971 was the first charitable contribution made to the association. Many more donations would follow.

Cay Beckmann was chairperson of a Twin Cities Art Council committee which brought "Artrain" to the area in 1972. "There's a definite interest in art here," says Beckmann. "Without art, there's nothing in life. The rewards are fantastic—just watching people's faces as they see something new, knowing how much the work is appreciated. Those are the rewards."

"Without art, there's nothing in life."

While Olga Krasl was association president in 1972, the group purchased a 100-year-old house at 600 State Street. Olga and George Krasl were instrumental in the acquisition which would provide a hub for the SJAA from 1972 to 1980. A dedication tea was held on February 18, 1972 and the art center was officially opened to the public. The international art collection of George and Olga Krasl was their first exhibition.

A dedication tea was held on February 18, 1972 and the art center was officially opened to the public.

A grand opening was held in 1973 with Olga Krasl serving a second term as president. This time the exhibition featured original drawings by Norman

Rockwell. Local artists gave demonstrations in the studio. Refreshments were served and a harpist performed.

With the center open on a limited basis, volunteers organized its management. Classes were offered, monthly exhibitions were hung and a volunteer organization called Friends of the Arts was formed to operate the center.

The 1973 art fair was attended by about 30,000 people who viewed the works of 150 artists. Proceeds from artist fees and program sales benefited the new center. The SJAA and "Friends" continued with monthly exhibitions, classes and fund raising. Community support for the center came from other groups as well as individuals outside the association. In 1974 the first recognition awards were presented to volunteers for their work. Heartha Whitlow earned a pin for donating the most hours.

The 1973 art fair was attended by 30,000 people who viewed the works of 150 artists.

Lucille Sabin was president during 1974 and 1975. And, in 1975, Gerry Tierney was hired as manager of the art center. In April, a gallery shop run by Cay Beckmann and Martha Lateulere was opened to give artists another place to display and sell their work.

Carol Ladrow was president in 1976 when the SJAA was named a beneficiary in a trust established by George J. Krasl, President of Leco Corporation and the Leco Plating Company in St. Joseph. Ladrow's term continued for two more years during which time the SJAA made plans to construct a new art center with funds from the trust. "We had always worked very hard," she recalled. "Volunteers could see that something was happening. The association was constantly improving, going ahead, not playing ring-around-the-rosy. I never had anybody say *no* when I asked for help at the center."

She asked Ed Conrad to head the Building and Site Committee for the new center. As an executive vice president at the NBD F & M Bank, Conrad had worked with the Krasls. "George and I had talked for years about building an art center. We had a couple of sites in mind and thought it would be a beautiful thing to have an art center on the bluff. With George gone, Olga encouraged me to take the job," Conrad said. "She loved the community. It was a pleasure to work with her."

Conrad chaired a committee including: Theodore Troff, Olga Krasl, Carol and Don Ladrow, Lucille Sabin, Margaret Hills, Ruth Iannelli and Leonard Schweitzer.

In 1976 the Michigan bicentennial was celebrated. Nancy Dandrea replaced Gerry Tierney as office manager. Building plans moved ahead. Choosing a name for the new structure was easy. Despite the many volunteers who contributed energy, expertise, funds and time to the SJAA, the 1979 Board of Directors, with Margaret Hills as president, unanimously approved the name Krasl Art Center (KAC) to acknowledge the contributions of George and Olga Krasl, whose trust fund made the center and its operation possible. At the time of the announcement, Olga said, "I'm happy to be able to do this—art was always one of my loves."

Olga said, "I'm happy to be able to do this—art was always one of my loves."

The ground-breaking ceremony in July marked the initial appearance of Alan Garfield, who assumed duties as center director on October 1, 1979. He resigned effective September 30, 1980. Also in July, Vicky Nemethy replaced Nancy Dandrea as office manager. She was named acting director when Garfield left.

Architects Perkins & Will of Chicago designed the center, Daverman Associates of Grand Rapids drew the working plans and construction documents. General contractor was Pearson Construction Company of Benton Harbor. Subcontractors were City Plumbing &

Heating Company of St. Joseph and Inter-City Electric of Benton Harbor. Four homes and an apartment building on Lake Boulevard and Pearl were demolished to make way for the center.

"We wanted a site that people could walk to, and it had to be in St. Joseph. George and Olga loved the community, and we liked the site on the bluff. It pleased Olga to no end with the beautiful view and the art fair right across the street."

"Our biggest problem was purchasing the property," says Conrad. "We wanted a site that people could walk to, and it had to be in St. Joseph. George and Olga loved the community, and we liked the site on the bluff. It pleased Olga to no end with the beautiful view and the art fair right across the street."

Margaret Hills, Building and Site Committee member and second term president of the SJAA in 1980, talked about volunteering in those days. She said, "During the planning stages, we located property, hired the architects, and went to the city commissioners and the planning commission for approval. We got to do more than volunteers would in a larger city. There they might be docents, but we did a little of everything."

With the bulk of the building fund coming from the Krasl trust, volunteers continued generating additional funds through memberships, classes, the gallery shop, the art fair, trips and other fund raising activities. According to Ed Conrad, "The overall investment was in the neighborhood of $1,600,000 including land, building construction, landscaping, furnishings and architectural fees." Eighteen major function areas within the center emphasized the primary goals of art exhibition and art education. At the dedication ceremonies in July, 1980, Olga Krasl said, "My philosophy is to make the world a little bit better because we have lived and what better way than to make something of beauty and joy."

"My philosophy is to make the world a little bit better because we have lived and what better way than to make something of beauty and joy."

Early in 1981 Dar Davis became the center's director and fifth paid administrator.

The KAC sponsored its first photography competition in 1981 and held events for children, teens and adults. Olga

View of Krasl's south wall from the parking lot.

Photo courtesy of Perkins & Will.

Krasl established a fund to provide ongoing musical programs for the center. The education department was founded with funds left by charter member Emily Parks Cooper, and Stephen and Betsy Upton donated funds for a printmaking studio. Marna Fisher was hired as education coordinator.

In 1982 the art fair was extended to two days to accommodate the growing crowds which filled Lake Bluff Park. An outdoor sculpture, *Nimbus Flight* by James Russell, was commissioned by private citizens for downtown St. Joseph and dedicated at the KAC. *(See photo in Chapter Seven.)*

An outdoor sculpture by James Russell was commissioned for St. Joseph and dedicated at the KAC.

The next year *Gulwave* was unveiled in the Krasl courtyard by sculptor Kirk Newman. With funds donated by Olga Krasl, *Gulwave* was designed to complement the art center building and to reflect the feeling of the area's natural landscape, the lake, the dunes and the birds. *Gulwave* was moved in 1989 to a site on the lawn where a birds-eye view of the work may be seen from the steps. *(See photo in Chapter Seven.)*

Also in 1983 the center was accredited by the American Association of Museums. Anne Stellwagen was hired as curator and the SJAA purchased a house at 708 State which they loaned to the

Fort Miami Heritage Society and to the St. Joseph Sesquicentennial Committee. The SJAA's first art center at 600 State had been sold to the Maud Preston Palenske Memorial Library and the city of St. Joseph. That house was demolished and replaced with a public park, which would later become the site of *Josephine*, an outdoor sculpture of a black bear and two cubs by Elke Krämer of Stuttgart, West Germany. The piece was installed in 1989.

Josephine, an outdoor sculpture of a black bear and two cubs by Elke Krämer of Stuttgart, West Germany, was installed in 1989.

St. Joseph's sesquicentennial year, 1984, saw many activities at the KAC in celebration of 150 years since the incorpo-

View of Krasl's west wall from Lake Boulevard.

ration of St. Joseph in 1834. The 23rd art fair drew record crowds of approximately 70,000.

In 1986 the outdoor sculpture collection was expanded to include a kinetic piece for the west wall of the center. It was entitled Three Lines Diagonal—Jointed, *by George Rickey.*

In 1986 the outdoor sculpture collection was expanded to include a kinetic piece for the west wall of the center. It was entitled *Three Lines Diagonal—Jointed* by George Rickey. The work was funded by KAC Friends of the Arts and local donors. Linda Monroe was hired as education coordinator.

The 25th anniversary of the St. Joseph Art Association and the annual art fair took place in 1987. During this time the Krasl Art Center had been a temporary home for international exhibits as well as shows by local artists. The SJAA continues to provide a variety of exhibits as well as art programs for people of all ages. In 1990, the group celebrated the tenth anniversary of the center.

Acknowledgment: Vicky Nemethy's work on "The Way We Were, St. Joseph Art Association, 1962-1987" for many of the facts about the SJAA.

Chapter

Seven

"How oft on its bank I have sunk in a dream,
Where the willows bent over me kissing the stream,
My boat with its nose sort of resting on shore,
While the cat-tails stood guarding a runaway oar;
It appeared like to me, that they sort of had some
Way of knowing that I would soon get overcome,
With the meadowlark singing just over the spot
I didn't care whether I floated or not—
Just resting out there for an hour or so
On the banks of the tranquil old River St. Joe."

Verse from "The River St. Joe"
by Ben King

A Sculpture Walk

Outdoor sculpture is part of our past and holds a place in our dreams for the future. Community leaders and groups have commissioned several pieces for public enjoyment. That tradition of sharing continues.

This sculpture walk encompasses an area that is easily accessible in less than an hour. Imagine the pieces from the comfort of your chair, or pick up this

Lake Bluff Park.

book and take a self-guided walking tour. As you walk, let your imagination wander to the many ideal sites where future sculpture might be placed.

The opportunities begin at the Krasl Art Center, 707 Lake Boulevard, where the building—with its copper roof stretching to the sky—is an architectural sculpture in itself. Built in 1980, the Krasl is the home of two outdoor works.

1. *Gulwave* by Kirk Newman of Kalamazoo, Michigan, is a six-foot bronze which the artist said "reflects the feeling of Krasl's environment on Lake Michigan and the gulls that swoop over the

Gulwave *by Kirk Neuman.*

shoreline." In 1983 it was installed in Krasl's courtyard near the front entrance. It was moved in 1989 to its present position on the lawn. Try to catch a birds-eye view of *Gulwave* to enjoy its shape from the top.

2. *Three Lines Diagonal—Jointed* by George Rickey, an internationally recognized artist living in East Chatham, New York, is a kinetic piece attached to the Krasl's west wall. The stainless steel lines move in the wind and never seem to form the same shapes twice. Krasl director Dar Davis said, "Someday Rickey will be as highly recognizable to the public as Henry Moore." The park bench in Lake Bluff Park across Lake Boulevard is recommended for viewing this piece. *(See photo in Chapter Six.)*

3. From the bench, note the bronze bust of Ben King, a nineteenth century writer who is said to be St. Joseph's most well-known poet and story teller. The first printing of his work appeared in 1898 and was printed twice that year and twice in the subsequent two years. By 1906, 13 volumes of his verses were in print. His memorial statue by Leonard Crunelle of Chicago was erected in 1924. *(See photo in Acknowledgments.)*

4. Further north, is a bronze statue of a World War I doughboy poised to hurl a

hand grenade. The statue is a replica stamped by the American Legion as the official doughboy statuary, and was the first official replica erected in Michigan. The memorial cost $1,800 and was dedicated on Armistice Day, November 11, 1930 as a memorial to all who served during the period now remembered as "the great war." The war itself lasted from 1914 to 1918, but United States involvement was only for one year, from 1917 to 1918. Mrs. Joseph (Mary) Clemens, whose son, Raymond, was killed in action, unveiled the statue which was dedicated to the city by the St. Joseph American Legion.

5. The Sesquicentennial Pavilion was erected in 1984 to honor St. Joseph's 150th birthday. Designed by John Allegretti, the pavilion was the focus of a year-long celebration headed by Priscilla Byrns and Judith Fowler, along with a large committee of volunteers. The people whose names appear on the imprinted bricks paid $25 per brick which funded the project estimated at $25,000. Unveiled on November 18, 1984, the pavilion is symbolic of the city motto "Holding on to the past, reaching out to the future."

1834-1984

Holding on to the past –
Reaching out to the future

6. The iron cannon next to the Broad Street stairwell bears the date 1864 and was unveiled in St. Joseph on July 4,

WW I Doughboy.

1897. A cannon ball is wedged in its nozzle to remind visitors of less peaceful times. Refinished in 1989, the cannon sits upon a fresh slab of concrete and sports an informative gilded plaque thanks to private citizen, John DeLapa.

In 1989 and 1990 a fund raising effort by another citizen, Fred Krause, restored two pyramids of cannon balls to their former site beside the cannon. Like the Sesquicentennial Pavilion, the cannon balls were paid for by private citizens who purchased them for $60 each. The refurbished site was dedicated to area citizens by St. Joseph Today and the United States Navy during a ceremony on Flag Day, June 14, 1990.

Sesquicentennial Pavilion 1834-1984.

Imprinted bricks sold for $25 to build the Sesquicentennial Pavilion.

7. *LaSalle's Monument* was placed in Lake Bluff Park in 1902 by the Algonquin Chapter of the Daughters of the American Revolution. Made of glacial stone found in the St. Joseph River by Captain

Cannon in 1988 before the restoration. The former 508 Broad Street building and the Elks Club are in the background.

1864 cannon and plaque taken on September 5, 1989.

142

Lloyd Clark of the United States Coast
Guard, it commemorates the landing of
Rene Robert Cavelier Sieur de LaSalle
in 1679, and the construction of Fort
Miami the same year.

*Glacial boulder erected in 1902 commemorates LaSalle's Land-
ing in 1679.*

The fort occupied the site of the present day Whitcomb Tower on the corner of Ship and Lake Boulevard. According to Mildred Webster and Fred Krause in their book *French Saint Joseph*, "They felled the trees that were on top of the hill and cleared away the bushes to provide a clearing for a fort that was forty feet long and eighty broad. It was constructed of great square pieces of timber, laid one upon the other. A great number of stakes, about twenty-five feet long were driven into the ground, providing protection on the river side. The building of this fort took up the month of November." Buried beneath the boulder is a time capsule containing memorabilia from 1902 including a newspaper, a history of LaSalle, photographs of St. Joseph, and a list of those who contributed to the memorial fund.

8. The 1934 boulder, known as the *Century Stone*, marks the centennial of St. Joseph's incorporation as a city. St. Joseph was listed as the third settlement in Michigan, dating from 1679. It has been a mission, a fortress, a trading post, a river port, a lake port, a fishing village, a fruit market, a health resort, and an industrial site. Buried beneath the Century Stone is a time capsule containing Centennial memorabilia, L. Benjamin Reber's *History of St. Joseph,* a list of community leaders, financial records, city documents, and a letter

from St. Joseph's mayor of 1934 to the mayor of 2034.

9. *Maids of the Mist* fountain was built in 1872 or 1873 by the J. W. Fiske Iron Works in New York City. Upon completion, it was shipped to Chicago where it became a part of the Inter-State Industrial Exposition from 1873 to 1891. It was moved in 1892 to St. Joseph by H. E.

Maids of the Mist.

Bucklen, then owner of the Whitcomb Hotel. The fountain's original cost was $5,000; it was purchased by Bucklen for around $500. The fountain was restored in 1974 by the city and the Fort Miami Heritage Society.

The *Maids of the Mist* quickly became a St. Joseph landmark popularly known as the "Stone Maidens." In the late 1930s, a local historian Calvin "Tad" Preston recalled that there once were fish and turtles in the pond around the fountain.

Preston gave each of the maids a name. He said the maid facing west—who in the past 60 years had witnessed the sails of old schooners from St. Joseph's booming lumber days and the smoke-belching stacks of passenger liners on Lake Michigan—was named Constance. The other maid was named Hope for the emotion which must have possessed her as she watched St. Joseph grow from a rowdy village of lumbermen and sailors to a quiet city with six municipalities branching out nearby.

10. *Pioneer Watch* a lookout point for early settlers, was formally installed with a railing and benches in 1939. It is easy to imagine how LaSalle and his men must have felt as they watched in vain from this point for the arrival of a forty-five ton sailboat, *Griffin* (also

Pioneer's Watch.

spelled Griffon, Griffen, Gryphon). Webster and Krause wrote that "the vessel disappeared on the return trip to Montreal. Waiting for the *Griffin* and its supplies was the small band of men who had come with LaSalle to the mouth of the St. Joseph River."

Days turned into months, but the ship never came. Finally they had to abandon the fort because there were no supplies and LaSalle feared his men might desert. On December 3, 1679 LaSalle led his men through the wilderness of present day northern Michigan to Canada where they were vulnerable to Indian attacks, wild animals, starvation, illness and the elements. They

View from Pioneer's Watch.

survived the journey, and the following year, in November, LaSalle returned to St. Joseph.

11. *Firemen's Monument* was erected in 1898 in memory of the men who died in the Yore Opera House fire in Benton Harbor in 1896. According to Robert Myers in *Historical Sketches of Berrien County*, a local clerk saw smoke coming from the building around midnight on the night of September 5 and 6. He sounded the alarm and Benton Harbor's firemen responded. Smoke and flames were pouring from the top floor of the four story building and could be seen across the river in St. Joseph. As the firemen battled, the blaze raged out of control and they feared it would spread to adjoining buildings.

The St. Joseph firemen were called to help and were directed into an alley to assist the Benton Harbor firemen already pouring water onto that side of the building. Moments after their arrival, a brick cornice broke loose and tons of brick fell on the men. Seven Benton Harbor and five St. Joseph firemen perished in the holocaust.

In honor of the dead, St. Joseph Fire Chief William Lindt arranged for fireman Fred Alden and five-year-old Mabel Snyder to pose for the statue which was

Firemen's Monument.

unveiled on Labor Day, 1898. A memorial was placed in Benton Harbor's Crystal Springs Cemetery in 1946 to honor that city's firemen.

12. The John E. N. Howard Bandshell, designed by Wayne Hatfield and Associates Architects, is named after the man who conducted the St. Joseph Municipal Band from 1947 to 1987. The open concrete bandshell, built in 1970, overlooks the mouth of the St. Joseph River and Lake Michigan.

Today, concerts are performed Sundays and holidays from late June to Labor Day at 3:30 and 7:30 p.m. There are few adjectives to describe the feeling of listening to familiar tunes played outdoors by a band of musicians. Add the fresh

John E. N. Howard Bandshell.

breezes off Lake Michigan and the sight of the panoramic western sky to the scene and we have what was once called "the best band concert in America."

13. *Sand Castles—What Dreams Are Made Of,* by Charles Parks of Wilmington, Delaware, is located below the bandshell in the Margaret Beckley Upton Arboretum. It is a bronze rendering of a father and two children dedicated in 1989 by the Upton Foundation in honor of Frederick S. Upton, husband of Margaret, and the co-founder of Whirlpool Corporation. Parks said, "Mr. Upton loved his family best of all, and for that love this work is dedicated to the citizens of St. Joseph." The Upton Foundation is led by the four children of Margaret and Frederick: Stephen, David, Priscilla and Sylvia.

Sand Castles: What Dreams Are Made Of *by Charles Parks.*

14. *Nimbus Flight* by James Russell of California is a 15-foot stainless steel piece on the corner of State and Pleasant Streets. It is designed to combine a feeling of birds in flight with the wind and waves of Lake Michigan. When it was unveiled in 1982 the artist said, "Art is basic to human existence. The aesthetic qualities of art make every event, place or thing develop identity, becoming meaningful and significant."

15. *Josephine* by Elke Krämer of Stuttgart, West Germany, was installed in 1989 in the park at State and Market

Nimbus Flight *by James Russell.*

153

Streets. The work was commissioned by the Old St. Joseph Neighborhood Preservation Association, funded by private donations, and completed with assistance from the Krasl Art Center. The bronze bear with a fish and two cubs recognizes the vital function of wildlife trapping and trading to the early establishment of cities here.

16. South on State Street, at the intersection of State and Main, is a pocket park containing a cast stone fountain depicting a boy and girl under an umbrella. The piece was planned by the Indian Hills Garden Club, installed by the city of St. Joseph, and presented to the citizens in 1940.

Josephine *by Elke Krämer.*

Fountain Square at State and Main Streets.

155

Sculpture forms.

Many more sculptures exist in south-western Michigan. At the Mercy-Memorial Medical Center on Napier Avenue, there is a colorful outdoor piece by Jim Clover. Inside, are works by Tuck Langland and Bill Cooper.

The Benton Harbor Public Library building was finished with small figures of Greek gods by Donald F. Snyder of Birmingham, Michigan, who also completed two interior pieces for the library.

In Niles, in a park beside the St. Joseph River, is a piece by Richard Hunt. At Southwestern Michigan College there are pieces by Marcia Wood and Jon Rush. Works by Alan Collins and Michael Todd are located at Andrews University.

The indoor sculptures that reside here are too numerous to mention. *Still Motion* by Jack Holme of Illinois, is located in the entryway of the new Peoples State Bank building on Pleasant Street and may be viewed through a window. Outside, in the brick plaza adjacent to the bank, is a sculpture pad waiting for a piece which is, as yet, unplanned.

Many more pieces exist in public and private establishments. Perhaps we'll guide you to them at another time.

Chapter

Eight

"Jane Jones said Abe Lincoln had no books at all
An' used to split rails when a boy;
An' General Grant was a tanner by trade
An' lived way out in Ill'nois.
So when the great war in the South first broke out
He stood on the side o' the right,
An' when Lincoln called him to take charge o' things,
He won nearly every blamed fight.
Jane Jones she honestly said it was so!
        Mebbe he did—
            I dunno!"

Verse from "Jane Jones"
by Ben King

Memorial Hall
and the
Curious Kids' Museum
by Rev. Christopher Momany and Jane Ammeson

September 1915 saw the dedication of Memorial Hall. The building was erected to stand for patriotic organizations of the area, but like most community endeavors, there was a history behind the project which predated its year of dedication. The real narrative began in 1865, some fifty years before the completion of the structure. The American Civil War was drawing to a close. On April 6, 1866, an organization of Union veterans known as the Grand Army of the Republic (GAR) was founded by Benjamin F. Stephenson in Decatur, Illinois.

Less than twenty years passed before the fraternal itch caught hold of the Union veterans in St. Joseph and Benton Harbor. The local post of the GAR was named the A. W. Chapman Post No. 21. The organization became a chartered entity on July 18, 1881 and was named after Captain Augustus W. Chapman, a St. Joseph man killed in action at Pleasant Hill, Louisiana, during the Civil War.

The post's charter members were not only upstanding citizens but also colorful veterans of the Union Army. Jay Drake, the first commander of the post was a former captain in the 7th Missouri Infantry. Thomas Botham, another charter member, was a fiery Irishman who fought for the Union, and legend claims single-handedly captured thirteen Confederates during one battle of the war.

Another charter member was a fiery Irishman who fought for the Union, and legend claims single-handedly captured thirteen Confederates during one battle of the war.

Perhaps one of the most prolific GAR participants here was Leonard J. Merchant, chosen quartermaster of the post in 1881. During his later years, Merchant would emerge as the Memorial Hall building project's number one supporter. The post grew in size and activity until its membership rolls included two hundred and forty-four names.

Rounding out the post were comrades who served as escorts during the funeral of Abraham Lincoln and members of the "Iron Brigade."

Warren Chapman, the father of A. W. Chapman, joined the post. While in uniform, the elder Chapman served as quartermaster under Major William Rufus Shafter, the man who would later lead the American forces in Cuba during the Spanish-American War. Rounding out the post were comrades who had served as escorts during the funeral of Abraham Lincoln while in the 24th Michigan Infantry, members of the famed "Iron Brigade," and men who fought with the 11th Michigan Cavalry when it captured the mounted escort of Confederate President Jefferson Davis.

From its beginning, the local GAR plunged into a plethora of activity. One of its efforts was the placing of a large naval cannon on the bluff, a monument which remains to this day. For years, the post hosted the annual meeting for Berrien County veterans of the Civil War, and the post's women's auxiliary, Logan Circle No. 11, Ladies of the GAR, also contributed to the community. Yet, for thirty-four years the local GAR had no building expressly built for veterans organizations.

One of its efforts was the placing of a large naval cannon on the bluff, a monument which remains to this day.

John A. Logan Circle No. 11, Ladies of the GAR.

Near the turn of the century, the need for a separate structure designated for patriotic groups became apparent. On February 13, 1896, an association to erect a memorial building was formed under the laws of the state of Michigan with the name The Memorial Hall Association of Berrien County. The first meetings of the association were held in Freund Brothers block of St. Joseph, which is where A. W. Chapman Post was meeting at this time.

There were ten original constituents of the association. Not surprisingly, many of them were also GAR men. Thomas Botham, C. H. Moulton, and L. J. Merchant were among those who led the original Memorial Hall Association. John Lane was elected president, but only one meeting was held. As the effort to raise construction funds proceeded, the president reported $30.00 collected, which was later increased to $60.25 by $1.00 subscriptions. The drive for funds stalled, and nothing further was done during the next seventeen years.

The Spanish-American campaign of 1898 supplied the area with a new generation of war veterans.

The Spanish-American campaign of 1898 supplied the area with a new generation of war veterans. Nationally, an organization of the United Spanish War Veterans was founded in 1898. The local group of Spanish-American War veterans was known as Ward Marrs Camp

No. 48, United Spanish War Veterans. These men gave a shot in the arm to veteran interests here. As it turned out, Ward Marrs Camp No. 48 was not officially represented in the Memorial Hall Association until January 28, 1924. But upon joining, the Spanish War Veterans immediately assumed an enterprising position in the activities of the association. James Wolf served as president from 1924 to 1927, and William Moore was in the thick of association activity while representing Ward Marrs Camp during the later 1920s.

As individuals, several area veterans of the Spanish-American War were involved in the history of Memorial Hall long before 1924. One in particular, Joseph Ogden Wells, proved to be a driving force in the association during the construction phase of the project. Earlier, while a soldier in Cuba, Wells served in Theodore Roosevelt's affluent "Rough Riders," winning extra mention for carrying off his wounded officer amid a storm of hostile bullets. As a Memorial Hall trustee during the building project, Wells was one of the few citizens to aid the association financially when operation of the structure was in its infancy. He is quoted in the records of the Memorial Hall Association as saying, "Call on me again if you need more help."

Wells served in Theodore Roosevelt's "Rough Riders," winning extra mention for carrying off his wounded officer amid a storm of hostile bullets.

The leading force behind the construction of the hall was Leonard J. Merchant.

While it is true that citizens such as Wells were a great help to the association, the leading force behind the construction of the hall was Leonard J. Merchant. During the Civil War, Merchant served in Company C of the 14 Connecticut Infantry. He distinguished himself as one of the most active members in the St. Joseph GAR. Merchant became involved in the newspaper business soon after his military service and lived for awhile in Benton Harbor before moving to St. Joseph in 1877. He bought the *Traveler-Herald* and renamed it the *St. Joseph Saturday Herald*. He piloted this paper until shortly after the turn of the century.

By 1913, L. J. Merchant had assumed leadership of the dormant drive to build a memorial building. He revived the effort and planned the strategy for raising funds. This gave rise to such encouraging donations that in September of 1914 a meeting of the association was called in which new officers were elected and further plans were made. Merchant, president of the association at this time, worked diligently to acquire a place for the building. A site was offered free for the structure in Benton Harbor, but Merchant declined the offer, preferring to find one in St. Joseph. Later that year, through personal contacts in Washington, L. J. Merchant received permission from the United States Government to lease a part of the old light house property in St. Joseph to the Memorial Hall Association of Berrien County. Work on the hall began in May of 1915, and the building was dedicated in September of the same year, "to stand not only for the Grand Army of the Republic and the cause for which its members fought but for other patriotic orders and all who helped found and preserve the United States of America."

Work on the hall began in May of 1915, and the building was dedicated in September of the same year.

When the building was dedicated, it was not fully ready for occupancy, and financial resources were scarce. The association struggled through the first few years and managed to keep the building operational, despite the sacrifices which came during 1917 and America's entrance into World War I. Following the war, in 1919, active charge of the building was turned over to Logan Circle of the GAR. This group offered to donate their services to maintain the hall.

Just as the ranks of the GAR were thinning, World War I provided the area with a young group of veterans who were in need of a place to hold meetings of their newly formed American Legion. Nationally, the legion was formed in Paris during March of 1919. Eleven local men died in the "war to end all

Eleven local men died in the "war to end all wars."

wars," and a large contingent of returning veterans met at Memorial Hall on September 23, 1919, to form Post No. 163 of the American Legion. Frederick S. Upton was chosen as the post's original commander. The first gathering was called and organized by Upton and J. D. Preston, and eventually the local post grew to have two hundred and fifty members. The legion remains a part of the American Legion of Michigan.

Not too many years after the American Legion was organized in St. Joseph, the Veterans of Foreign Wars (VFW) founded a local post. Post No. 206 of the VFW was chartered on August 3, 1926, with an original membership of sixty-five. This was not the only VFW organization to use Memorial Hall. As the 1920s were drawing to a close, the memorial building was firmly established as a key gathering place for local veterans and their respective groups.

The memorial building was firmly established as a key gathering place for local veterans and their respective groups.

By the early and mid-1930s, ownership of the land Memorial Hall stands on passed from the hands of the United States government to the city of St. Joseph. The building itself passed from the Memorial Hall Association to the U. S. government and then, with the land, onto the city of St. Joseph.

At the close of 1935, the Memorial Hall Association took steps to become an incorporated entity. Officially the association was designated as being "composed of representatives from the various patriotic organizations holding regular meetings in the Memorial Hall...who shall manage the building for the benefit of all such organizations..."

Local use of the structure followed a course of business as usual until war clouds in Europe and the Pacific promised to rouse the patriotism of America once more. As in all other conflicts, World War II struck deeply into our community. In 1946 many of these men pioneered a local post of American Veterans of World War II, known as AMVETS. Nationally, the organization was begun in 1944 and chartered by Congress in 1947. The local gathering of AMVETS was chartered as Post No. 88 and has enjoyed the services of many highly respected individuals. Among these is Mr. Tom Sparks, former Mayor of St. Joseph.

As in all other conflicts, World War II struck deeply into our community.

In 1956 another organization joined the ranks of those already using the hall. This time it was not a young group of servicemen returning from recent conflict but rather, a group of World War I veterans who felt the need to start their own brotherhood. This band, known as Barracks No. 582 of the Veterans of World War I, was chartered in 1956 with sixty members. Through the labors of two citizens, Lyle Furlong and Julius A. Reischke, Barracks No. 582 grew to include more than one hundred.

The last member of the GAR, C. B. Holmes, stands between Nelson Wood and James Brant.

While it is true that Memorial Hall has revolved around veterans' organizations, the structure has also been used by other civic groups. Some of these are the Daughters of Union Veterans, a dog obedience school, a karate school, the Royal Neighbors, St. Joseph Chapter of the Deaf, the Sons of Norway, Volvo Lodge, the Rebekahs, and Benton Lodge No. 132 of the Odd Fellows.

By the scales of world history, Memorial Hall's 75 years might be an inconsequential stretch of time. But that period represents two world wars, much regional conflict, and now, the closure to a long season of cold war. For the Twin Cities area, these years have borne witness to tremendous local change.

That period represents two world wars, much regional conflict, and now, the closure to a long season of cold war. For the Twin Cities area, these years have borne witness to tremendous local change.

What we have in Memorial Hall is a bridge in time which manages to catch past remnants of blue and gray, while also extending eloquently into the future. The humble sentinel above the lake exemplifies a long line of American servicemen.

In 1988 the city of St. Joseph began negotiations with members of the newly formed Curious Kids' Museum who wanted to use Memorial Hall as their headquarters. "I wanted the children in our community to be able to have the same access to learning and experi-

"I wanted the children ...to be able to have the same access to learning and experimenting that children in bigger cities have."

171

menting that children in bigger cities have," says Mary Baske, founder.

The learning experience that Baske, a mother of three, was thinking about could be found in a hands-on children's museum. The problem was, St. Joseph didn't have one and the nearest children's museum was hours away.

Baske introduced the idea at a dinner party she held in December of 1987. By the following month, an exploratory committee had formed to determine the feasibility of such an organization. Public reaction was mixed, but that didn't stop Baske. For every person she met who told her "great idea, but it'll never work" she convinced two more that it was the best idea in the world.

But there's a big step between convincing people that you have a good idea and actually opening a museum's doors.

But there's a big step between convincing people that you have a good idea and actually opening a museum's doors. Baske, who had been a teacher for emotionally impaired youngsters, didn't know the first thing about raising grant money or soliciting funds from individuals, groups and businesses. She and her friends learned quickly.

People who served on the board of trustees include Mary Baske, Elizabeth Garey, Claudia Vescolani, Elizabeth Upton, T. J. Passaro, Jane Ammeson,

172

Edward Meny, David Ellis, Julie Keller, Jeanette Leahey, Linda Monroe, Dr. Anne Mulder, Thomas MacFarlane, George Barfield, Kenneth Kaminski, Mary McKisson, Edward Strach and Jack Edinger.

Advisory council members have included Dennis Albee, Cynthia Bewick, Mary Buckleitner, Dr. Gale Cutler, Anne McCausland, James Pinkerton, Dr. David Ratajik, David Ross, Shelley Upton, Kathryn Zerler, Patrick Moody, William Rudman, Lynne Christiano, Renee Williams, Kristi O'Dorisio and Keith Stevens.

Income for starting the museum came primarily from the community. Museum supporters enlisted the financial support of area corporations, civic groups, foundations and individuals. Once started, however, the museum generates revenues from admissions, memberships and special events. In addition, city, state and federal grants are being utilized. Investment opportunities in the museum include sponsoring an exhibit, underwriting the cost of an educational program, assisting with the printing of projects or importing special speakers.

The group looked for a building that met certain specifications including a mini-

Income for starting the museum came primarily from the community.

The hall was in need of extensive renovations, but through generous donations, it has been completely revamped while still keeping its integrity.

mum of 3,000 square feet with rooms with higher ceilings for many of the science exhibits. Location was also important so that patrons could easily reach the museum. That's why Memorial Hall, with its 4,000 square feet, seemed so ideal to house the museum. Its location follows the cultural vanguard already established along that street by the Krasl Art Center and the Maud Preston Palenske Memorial Library. The hall was in need of extensive renovations, but through generous donations, it has been completely revamped while still

Memorial Hall and the Curious Kids' Museum at 415 Lake Boulevard.

keeping its integrity. Architect Christopher Brooks donated much time and energy to the revitalization. The museum was made barrier free with the addition of an elevator.

It was the goal of the museum to employ a minimum amount of staff and to rely upon volunteers to keep the doors open. The volunteer guild includes people from retired educators, artists, carpenters, high school and college students to lawyers and doctors.

When Baske first decided to establish a hands-on children's museum in St. Joseph, she had no idea how successful it would turn out to be. The museum opened in September of 1989, less than two years after that introductory dinner party. In the first eleven months of operation, 37,000 visitors passed through the museum and within ten months museum membership reached three hundred.

It opened in September, 1989, less than two years after that introductory dinner party. In the first eleven months of operation, 37,000 visitors passed through the museum.

An old Chinese proverb says:
I hear and I forget.
I see and I remember.
I do and I understand.

That's the credo of the Curious Kids' Museum because doing is often the most important aspect of learning. Think about how you learned to tie your

Doing is often the most important aspect of learning.

shoelaces, scramble an egg or drive a car. Did you learn by reading directions? No. You learned by watching and by trying it for yourself.

What is the Curious Kids' Museum? Well, you won't find any echoing hallways, glass cases, grumpy guards or "don't touch signs" in this museum. Most children's museums, including the Curious Kids', don't have valuable collections the way grown-up museums do. Instead, the museum concentrates on special displays that explain how the world works. A children's museum is designed especially for children from two to thirteen years old and gives free rein to their inquiring hands and minds. It's an environment where families and school groups learn about the arts, sciences and humanities. A children's museum is fun, and it cultivates the curious mind. Currently, there are approximately 400 hands-on museums in the country. *Newsweek* magazine describes the growth of children's museums to be spreading almost as fast as Pizza Huts since the first, the Brooklyn Children's Museum, was founded in 1899.

A children's museum is designed especially for children from two to thirteen years old and gives free rein to their inquiring hands and minds.

The Memorial Hall portion of this chapter was written by the Reverend Christopher Momany who is a native of St. Joseph and currently serves as pastor of the New Hope United Methodist Church, Mecosta, Michigan. The museum section was written by Jane Ammeson who is a practicing psychologist and a free-lance writer living in Stevensville, Michigan.

176

Chapter

Nine

"I've seen folks gether thare in crowds
Jist fer to watch the golden clouds
Changin' shapes, and sort o' windin'
Into figgers, never mindin'
That old lake spread out below,
Reflectin' 'em at Old St. Joe."

Verse from "Old St. Joe"
by Ben King

Downtown St. Joseph:
1979-1989
A Decade of Development

For more than 150 years, St. Joseph has offered consumers specialty merchandise, professional services and fine dining in a lakeside environment of charm and grace. St. Joseph is old enough to know that reputations take years to build, money is earned by hard work, and quality is forever. Here, the tradition of courtesy and heirloom value is a community legacy.

Old Commercial National Bank on southeast corner of State and Pleasant Streets in 1920s. Booth at left was occupied by the police department.

Like the state of Michigan, downtown St. Joseph is surrounded on three sides by water.

Like the state of Michigan, downtown St. Joseph is surrounded on three sides by water. This proximity to both a deep water port and recreational beaches makes the water resources an integral part of local commerce. Fishing and boating industries thrive year around.

The central business district consists of specialty shops with merchandise ranging from men, women and children's apparel, jewelry and accessories, to books, china and hand-made gifts. Many stores offer complimentary gift wrapping, shipping services and special ordering. Convenience is often just a

Corner of State and Broad Streets looking north down State in about 1900.

telephone call away, but many customers prefer to drive downtown and park at the doorsteps of the quaint shops.

In 1976 city entrepreneurs took a critical look and decided that the downtown area was beginning to show the effects of age. Like many downtowns, the parallel parking, high street lights and cracked sidewalks dated from the early 1900s. It seemed unnatural for a community with so many parks elsewhere to be devoid of greenery in the business district. To address the updating of the commercial district, city commissioners formed the Downtown Development Authority (DDA) and things began to change.

In 1976 city entrepreneurs took a critical look and decided that the downtown area was beginning to show the effects of age.

... and things began to change.

On November 15, 1976 the following men became charter members of the DDA: Jack Sparks, John Fetters, Richard Schanze, Ray Carlson, Theodore Bestervelt, LeRoy Hornack, Clifford Emlong, George Keller. Others who have served on the DDA include: Alice Donaldson, Michael Cook, Leroy Selent, Mark Bowman, John Miner, Douglas Landis, Edgar Ross.

Ronald S. Momany, as the community development coordinator for the city of St. Joseph, served as the executive director of the DDA from its inception in 1976 to November 20, 1985. When Momany became clerk/finance director for the city in 1985, he turned over his duties as executive director of the DDA to Norman Oorbeck who currently holds the position. Momany continues to serve the DDA as its treasurer.

By the late 1970s historic renovations were started downtown...

By the late 1970s historic renovations were started on downtown streets which resulted in the St. Joseph of the 1980s— a modernized combination of city life with the freshness of a location on the bluffs of Lake Michigan.

State Street sidewalk reconstruction in downtown St. Joseph in 1979. Note the paving brick on Broad Street in the foreground, the old pole-top luminaries and the new double-bulbed decorative lighting.

Left to right: St. Joseph city commissioners Warren Gast, John Gessert, Joseph Hanley, William Gillespie, and Downtown Development Authority chairman George Keller participate in dedication of the State Street reconstruction project in downtown St. Joseph.

View of the west side of the 200 block of State Street after renovations in the early 1980s.

Based on the theme "A Special Place on the Lake," St. Joseph developed its qualities of peacefulness, friendliness, beauty and turn-of-the-century amenities.

Based on the theme "A Special Place on the Lake," St. Joseph developed its qualities of peacefulness, friendliness, beauty and turn-of-the-century amenities. Two-way streets became one-way with angle parking on one side only. The old brick streets were retained. Sidewalks were widened with a buff-colored concrete, Linden trees were planted and then protected with flat, decorative grates inserted flush with the walks. Double-bulbed street lights called Coney Island lights were installed along with matching woven-wire flower planters, litter barrels, bollerts and wooden benches. The decorative components work with the 19th and 20th century buildings to provide an atmosphere of warmth in the business environment.

First, State Street was renovated, then Pleasant Street, then the central parking lots, alleyways and Broad Street. Next, the Office District on the east side of Main Street was redone. Elm Street and the parking lots near the Boulevard Hotel were improved and landscaped. The Margaret B. Upton Arboretum was extended along Vine Street. Future plans include development of land between Lake Bluff Park and Silver Beach.

Building owners were given "ideal" artistic renderings depicting how their buildings could best assimilate with the public renovations. Today, many private sector interests have complied with these suggestions. Notable improvements include front and rear customer entrances for convenient access to the resurfaced parking lots.

In addition to forming the DDA for the purpose of administering the funds for bricks and mortar, community leaders organized St. Joseph Today (SJT) in 1979 to provide promotional activities to bring people into the city.

EXPERIENCE ST. JOSEPH TODAY

SJT works with the DDA to advance the interest of retailers, property owners, business and professional people, and consumers in the business districts of St. Joseph. Activities include advertising, promotions, publicity and public relations on behalf of the city. SJT is not a part of city government. It is a non-profit agency which raises its funds from membership contributions.

Jack Sparks, former president and CEO of the Whirlpool Corporation and a charter DDA member, was instrumental in the early success of SJT. Its first director was Len Hardke, a loaned executive whose salary was paid by Whirlpool. The original offices were located in the old Peoples State Bank building at the corner of Ship and State Streets. Rent for the space was donated

Its first director was Len Hardke, a loaned executive whose salary was paid by Whirlpool.

by the bank. Hardke was executive director from 1979 to 1981, Patti Sizer was executive director from 1981 to 1984, and Kathryn Zerler, the present executive director, was appointed on September 17, 1984.

Charter members of the SJT Advisory Council were: John Stubblefield, Mayor Franklin Smith, William Sinclair, C. Stuart Siebert, Richard Schanze, George Keller, John Globensky, Clifford Emlong, Roger Curry and Jon Capron. Others who have served on the council include: Theodore Bestervelt, Robert Gerbel, Thomas McCaffrey, Fredda Sparks, Joseph and Marjorie Clemens, Warren Gast, Theodore Bachunas, Betty

Left to right: Sylvia Upton Wood, Fredda and Jack Sparks enjoy a Brown Bag Concert in Lake Bluff Park.

The summer concerts are popular with parents, children, business people and seniors.

Horse-drawn trolley rides by Bennett's Belgians have become an institution in St. Joseph. The rides are sponsored by the Upton Foundation and coordinated by St. Joseph Today.

Mashke, Lenard Schweitzer, Marie Franz, Edward Conrad, LuAnn Mashke, George Wardeberg and Jay Van Den Berg.

St. Joseph Today is an active member of the Twin Cities Area Chamber of Commerce, the Southwestern Michigan Tourist Council, the West Michigan Tourist Association, and the Tourism Advisory Council to Congressman Fred Upton.

When speaking about the success of St. Joseph other factors play critical roles. First, the cooperation initiated by the city commission in 1976 continues to-

The St. Joseph Today logo is used on banners at special events.

day. The commission, the DDA and SJT often work together to solve problems and plan events.

The commission, DDA and SJT often work together.

The logo is used to indicate St. Joseph Today members who display this decal in their windows.

The logo is used on street banners to welcome people to St. Joseph.

Of equal importance is information exchange, both formally and informally. Keeping lines of communication open between all groups is vital. Through its Community Calendar, SJT is able to work with many community-based organizations and Lake Michigan College to encourage and promote participation in local events and activities.

Next, the St. Joseph Improvement Association, which was started by John Stubblefield, former president of the Peoples State Bank, plays an active part in property acquisition for the purpose of serving the city with decisions as to the most favorable use of land. The Twin Cities Area Chamber of Commerce, with representation on the SJT Advisory Board, is also involved in ongoing activities.

The St. Joseph city motto reflects this image of cooperation. It says, "Holding on to the past, reaching out to the future." It is this juxtaposition of the old and the new, the public and the private sectors together, which makes the city of St. Joseph unique.

The following photographs were taken in downtown St. Joseph during the 1950s.

Of equal importance is information exchange, both formally and informally.

"Holding on to the past, reaching out to the future."

Downtown St. Joseph in the 1950s had parallel parking with meters and deteriorating buildings. These buildings on the east side of the 100 block of State Street were demolished. This is the current site of the St. Joseph Holiday Inn parking lot.

View of corner of State and Ship Streets looking east down Ship.

The southwest corner of State and Ship Streets was the site of the former Herring Sporting Goods Store. Today it is a parking lot owned by the Peoples State Bank.

View of east side of 200 block of State Street.

Northeast corner of State and Pleasant Streets.

Southwest corner of State and Pleasant Streets was formerly called the Shepard-Benning Building. It is now called the Keller Building. The upstairs corner shown here is the office of St. Joseph Today.

View of the 300 block of State Street on the west side.

View of east side of 300 block of State Street.

Northeast corner of State and Broad Streets shows Rimes and Hildebrand before renovations.

View of east side of 400 block of State Street.

Northeast corner of State and Elm Streets.

*Southwest corner of State and Broad Streets includes this large
building owned by the Elks Club.*

West side of 400 block of State Street includes the Duncan Block on the corner.

Chapter

Ten

"Of all the towns that jest suits me
From Stevensville to Manistee,
There's one old place I can't fergit;
It ain't a great ways off, and yit
From here it's sixty miles or so
In a bee line—that's Old St. Joe."

Verse from "Old St. Joe"
by Ben King

A Downtown Walking Tour

The reader is invited to take this book for a walk through downtown St. Joseph. Once there, look up and enjoy the architecture that is a part of our past.
(See map on next page)

1. Beginning at State and Pleasant, note the SJS Federal Savings Bank building, which dates from the early 1900s. It is an example of classical revival commercial architecture. One significant feature is the front facade of stonework with stone dentils and relief carvings over the door. Doric columns frame the modernized entrance, and an extended clock with bronze frame displays the time on all four sides.

2. Across Pleasant Street is a stainless-steel sculpture resembling a giant bird in flight. Entitled *Nimbus Flight*, it was completed by James Russell in 1982. It is one of several outdoor sculptures which are included in Chapter Seven of this book.

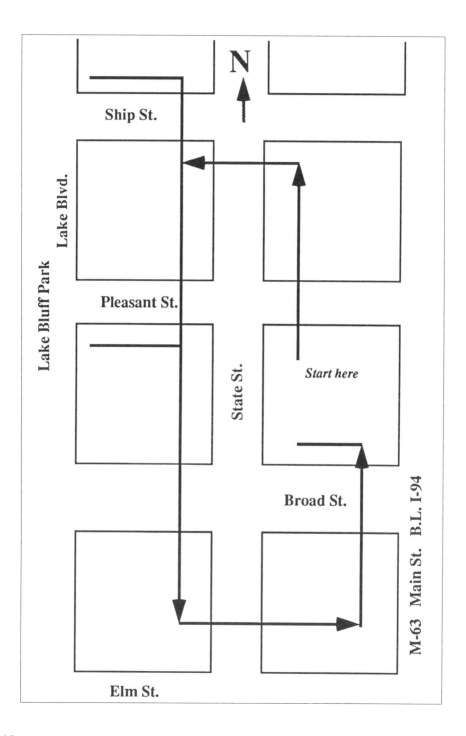

Walking Through
Downtown St. Joseph

3. Walking north on State, H.I.'s Saloon and The Mole Hole at 214 and 212, respectively, were once one building dating from the early 1900s. The Mole Hole was modernized by John and Barbara Soos in 1987, including front and rear customer entrances and an apartment overhead. H.I.'s Saloon, owned by Henry and Martha Ingier, has become a tourist attraction in itself with a colorful show of lights for every season.

4. One of Montgomery Ward's first stores was located at 209 State. He was born in Niles, Michigan.

5. Nuechterlein's Camera Shop, on the corner of Ship and State, was established by Warren "Doc" Nuechterlein in 1930 on the second story of 204 State Street. Now managed by his son, Warren, it has been a part of business in St. Joseph for more than half a century.

6. The old Peoples State Bank building—kitty-corner from Nuechterlein's—circa 1912, is classical revival architecture with a domed tower, ionic columns, and curved entrance with carvings. The historic plaque on the side of the building identifies this site as the former end of old Territorial Road.

7. Looking west, on the corner of Ship and Lake Boulevard, is the Whitcomb

Tower, formerly the Whitcomb Hotel. The hotel held its grand opening in 1928. Featuring mineral baths, a talkative parrot named Polly, elegant dinner dances, Sunday brunches and the "Marine Bar," this hotel was a popular spot.

You are invited to visit the parlor and view a mural steeped in local history. The panels depict Father Jacques Marquette and explorer Louis Joliet in birch bark canoes paddling Lake Michigan. The mural was presented on opening day, May 3, 1928 by the Women's Chamber of Commerce as a gift to the city. Today, the Whitcomb Tower is a retirement residence.

8. The parking lot on the corner of Ship and State next to 204 State was the site of the Herring Sporting Goods store. Mr. Herring flew a plane on Silver Beach before the Wright brothers. Herring was airborne for eight to ten seconds and traveled about 100 feet. In the final analysis, his plane was considered a glider not an airplane, so the Wright brothers went down in history instead. A model of Herring's plane is in the lobby of the Twin Cities Airport terminal in Benton Harbor.

9. In the early 1900s, Richter's Hardware Store was located at 218 State. Today, Carroll Crafts, owned by Dale and

Marian Hogue, has front and rear customer entrances and a beautiful tin ceiling.

10. Gillespie's has been a drug store since 1866. Frank Gillespie arrived in 1905 and bought the business. Four of his six children became pharmacists: Collins, Robert, and William worked in the downtown store; and Richard opened his own drug store in south St. Joseph. The building at 220 State was remodeled in the 1920s after the California commercial style of architecture. Over the entrance, note the stone decorations and the stained-glass frieze (which may be seen better from inside the building). It is now owned by Ronald and Cheryl Beck.

Gillespie's interior in 1950.

During the State Street renovations in 1979, a time capsule was buried by Collins and William Gillespie. Located eight feet from the State Street entrance and two feet to the north, the time capsule contains items such as a Susan B. Anthony dollar, a newspaper, and a Timex watch. Bill said, "We wanted to see if the watch would keep on ticking."

11. Dr. Frank Deitch once had an office located above 222 State. He would make a set of upper and lower teeth for $5.00.

12. In the early 1900s, the Shepard-Benning Building—now the Keller Building on the southwest corner of State and Pleasant—was the home of Shepard & Benning Company, a clothing store featuring New York and Paris fashions. One of their ads read, "Clothes are like people—they are judged not by their looks, but by what they do or don't do."

13. The YWCA of Southwestern Michigan received its charter in 1911. The original group met in rooms over what is now the G. C. Murphy Company at 307 State. The cornerstone of the colonial red brick structure at 508 Pleasant Street was laid in 1925 and the building was dedicated on Easter Sunday, 1926.

An addition was built in 1958, including a commercial kitchen and fireside lounge to promote youth activities. The building houses a full-size swimming pool and gymnasium.

14. The Chan's Garden restaurant building was built in the late 1800s. An example of 19th century Queen Anne commercial style, note the second story bay which is ornate with rosettes and tall, narrow windows with pedimented lintels and appliqued details.

This building once housed the Lucker Meat Market, an old-fashioned butchery with sawdust covering the floor. Lucker was a notorious town character who became agitated by the incessant ringing of a crank-type telephone. In a fit of anger, he pulled the phone off the wall and threw it onto State Street.

15. G. C. Murphy Co. in the State Building at 307 State hasn't changed in years. It is a favorite store in St. Joseph. People love the old wooden floors which creak, and the feeling that one can enter the store with a nickel and come out with a bag full of candy. The department store carries everything from kitchenware, to cosmetics, gardening supplies, toys and hardware. Murphy's moved to its present location in 1939. It was formerly at 306 State where the Lemon Tree is now located.

16. The Sand Box, owned by Sheila Grossman, at 318 State, is part of the Rice Block. Note the windows on the second story which connect this building with 320 State. Step inside and look at the fine tin ceiling dating from around the turn-of-the-century.

17. Helaine's Inc., at 320 State is also part of the Rice Block. This 19th century Italian Renaissance Revival building was built in 1897 and once had a cupola. Still remaining is the corner bay window with its ornate details of festoons, rosettes and brackets. Note the tall, narrow windows on the second and third stories. Hillard and Sharon Friedman restored the building in 1986.

18. Troost Brothers Furniture store is located in the Century Building at 403 State. Built in 1901, this Queen Anne structure is in original condition on the upper floors. Owners Ted and Peggy Bestervelt invite you to go upstairs and look. It has two towers and four bays with pattern work such as checkerboard, polka dot, diamond, zigzag and square dentils. The arched brickwork reflects 19th century Richardson Romanesque architecture. Troost Brothers has been in St. Joseph since 1923.

19. The Duncan Block at the corner of Elm and State was built by John Duncan.

One of his ads read, "Do you ever take a day off? Wouldn't it be a good stunt for you to step into John F. Duncan's Hardware Department Store and buy yourself a catching mitt and ball? Or buy a pair of dumb bells or a fishing tackle outfit or a punching bag or a set of boxing gloves or Indian clubs and a golf outfit or a tennis outfit or a croquet set or any old thing to play with? GET BUSY."

20. On the opposite side of State was the Caldwell Theatre where many residents viewed Saturday morning "thrillers" usually to be continued from week to week. Joe Louis, long-reigning heavyweight boxing champion, was frequently seen at the Caldwell. He stayed at his trainer's home in Stevensville for sev-

Corner of State and Elm Streets with the Boulevard Hotel in the background.

eral months out of the year during the late 1930s.

21. The grey house on Elm Street next to the former library at 500 Main Street is known as the first Captain Wallace House, built in the mid-1800s. It is a rare vernacular example of Gothic revival style architecture. Note the steep pitched roof with its curved bargeboard applique work under the eaves and the narrow windows with their triangular pediment and keystone on top. The original clapboard remains intact, but the porch with its Gothic details has been removed. Rumor has it that during a funeral once held in the house, the casket suddenly fell through the floorboards.

Southwest corner of Elm and Main Streets is a former Andrew Carnegie library, now the site of Allegretti Architects.

22. Five Hundred Main, at the corner of Main and Elm, is the former public library. Built in 1904 with a $10,000 grant from Andrew Carnegie, it is an example of classical revival architecture with eclectic elements. Note the curved corner entrance with its iron railings, high steps, ionic columns and door with sidelights. Also note the curved stone balustrade with indented brackets and the curved rear section. The building was a library until 1964. It was purchased in 1982 by John Allegretti of Allegretti Architects, who invites you to view the interior of the upper level.

23. The Michigan Bell Telephone building, at 415 Main, was built in 1926. The Bureau of History under the Michigan Department of State feels that this building is a fine example of art deco architecture with its yellow brick, red tile roof, arched indented windows and doors, and arched brick treatment in the cornice. Marilyn Schanze bought the building from James DeVries and renovated it in 1988.

24. City Hall at 620 Broad Street houses the police and fire stations as well as city administrative offices. In the days of the horse-drawn fire wagons, the fire station served as a stable and hay for the horses was stored overhead. Even today, on occasion, a bit of hay still falls from

City Hall in 1990.

City Hall in 1894.

the ceiling. The department was motorized in 1916.

When the Whitcomb Hotel closed in 1966, the owners gave the firemen their parrot. A gregarious old bird, Polly quickly became the firemen's friend. When she died a few years later, the firemen buried her behind the *Firemen's Monument* in Lake Bluff Park just across the street from the Whitcomb.

25. Rimes Inc., formerly Rimes & Hildebrand, on the corner of State and Broad at 323 State, has been in business since the 1890s. Still owned and operated by the Rimes family, this department store has been a center of commerce in St. Joseph for nearly a century.

This chapter, written with architectural assistance by Michele Spencer, has been reproduced as a brochure for the city of St. Joseph.

Annotated Bibliography
by Barbara G. Troost

For additional information consult these materials found in the Maud Preston Palenske Memorial Library, 500 Market Street, St. Joseph, Michigan.

Aldrich, Burton R., *A History of the Schools of St. Joseph, Michigan,* Burton Aldrich, 1981.
    A paper prepared for Fort Miami Heritage Society.

Baker, Helen C., *The Story of the Baker-Vawter Company,* Helen C. Baker, 1970.
    History taken from interviews with Will Vawter.

Benton Harbor, Michigan, Benton Harbor Improvement Association, 1891.
    Photographs and information about early Benton Harbor businesses and industries.

Maud Preston Palenske Memorial Library.

Benton Harbor, the Metropolis of the Michigan Fruit Belt, Leader Publishing Company, 1915.
   Photographs and information about people, homes and businesses in Benton Harbor during the early part of the century.

Carney, James T., *Berrien Bicentennial,* Berrien County Bicentennial Commission, 1976.
   Brief histories of the county, townships, cities and villages.

A Century of Faith: St. Joseph Catholic Church, St. Joseph, Michigan 1865-1965, St. Joseph Catholic Church, 1966.
   Photographs and information about the people, organizations and history of this church.

Champion, Ella, *Berrien's Beginnings,* Ad/Print Company, 1926.

Chauncey, A. E., *Berrien County, A Nineteenth Century Story,* Burch Printers, Benton Harbor, 1955.

Coolidge, Judge Orville W., *A Twentieth Century History of Berrien County, Michigan,* Lewis Publishing Company, Chicago, 1906.

Ellis, Franklin, *History of Berrien and Van Buren Counties, Michigan,* D. W. Ensign and Company, 1880.

Fogarty, Robert S., *The Righteous Remnant: the House of David,* Kent State University Press, Kent, Ohio, 1981.
   Scholarly study of the House of David.

From Times Past, Leco Corporation, St. Joseph, 1986. Reprinted from *Michigan History Magazine,* July/August, 1979.

Histories of Silver Beach, St. Joseph, and House of David, Benton Harbor. Includes "Silver Beach: A Scrapbook of Summers Past" by Alan Schultz, and "House of David: Hoax or Heaven?" by Roger L. Rosentreter.

Havira, Barbara Speas, *Factories and Workers in Three Michigan Towns 1880-1920,* dissertation (Ph.D), Michigan State University, East Lansing, 1986.

Cooper Wells Hosiery Company of St. Joseph is one of the factories studied in this doctoral dissertation.

Headlight Flashes, Chicago Railroad Publishing Company, July, 1898.

A railroad magazine containing photographs and paragraphs about well-known St. Joseph/Benton Harbor people, businesses and industries of 1898.

Heath Stories: From Ed Heath and Howard Anthony to the Present, two volumes compiled by Bjorn Heyning, St. Joseph, 1986.

An historical and architectural overview.

Historic Sites of Berrien County, Michigan historical research by Harold A. Atwood, Berrien Community Foundation, St. Joseph, 1989.

Includes map.

An Historical and Architectural Overview of the Old St. Joseph Historic District, Old St. Joseph Neighborhood Preservation Association, 1981.

Describes a number of homes in the historic district.

History: Lake Michigan College, 1946-1976, 1976.

History of the F. P. Rosback Company 1881-1981, Rosback Company, 1981.

McConnell, Edith W., *A History of St. Paul's Episcopal Church in St. Joseph, Michigan 1835-1987,* two volumes revised February 1962. Photocopy of typescript edition, St. Joseph, 1988.
    A brief history of the early church followed by weekly reports of events.

McConnell, Madeleine, *The Diary of Madeleine McConnell, July 1918-February 1919,* typescript transcribed from the original by Shirley Evans Robbins, Albuquerque, New Mexico, 1988.
    Diary of a World War I Army nurse (St. Joseph resident).

Momany, Chris, *Memorial Hall: A Bridge in Time,* summary prepared for the city of St. Joseph, Michigan. City of St. Joseph, 1982.
    History of this St. Joseph building and veterans.

Morton, J. S., *Reminiscences of the Lower St. Joseph River Valley,* The Federation of Women's Clubs, Benton Harbor, A. B. Morse Company.

Moulds, Catherine, *Chips Fell in the Valley 1650-1963,* University Press, Berrien Springs, 1963.
    A history of the St. Joseph and Benton Harbor area written for young people.

Myers, Robert C., *Historical Sketches of Berrien County,* volumes 1 and 2, The 1839 Courthouse Museum, Berrien Springs, 1988, 1989.
  The sketches were originally written and presented for "Art Talk" on WAUS Radio at Andrews University in Berrien Springs.

100 Years of Service, First Congregational Church of St. Joseph, 1954.
  The story of the founding and development of this church.

Palenske, Fred C., *Recollections of Fred C. Palenske,* ed., A. G. Preston, Jr., St. Joseph, Michigan, 1987.
  Typescript of oral interview conducted by C. Moulton Davis and Lewis Filstrup for Fort Miami Heritage Society, 1968.

Pender, James, *History of Benton Harbor and Tales of Village Days,* Braun Publishing Company, Chicago, 1915.
  Short chapters about Benton Harbor in early days.

Preston, A. G. Jr., *Berrien County's Courthouses,* Maud Preston Palenske Memorial Library, 1978.

Preston, A. G. Jr., *The Banks of St. Joseph,* A. G. Preston, Jr., St. Joseph, 1982.

Preston, A. G. Jr., *A Political History of St. Joseph,* A. G. Preston, Jr., St. Joseph, 1977.

Preston, A. G. Jr., *The Story of St. Joseph, Michigan,* Fort Miami Heritage Society, St. Joseph, 1972.

Preston, Harriet N., *The Story of Ann Jenette Loomis Preston and Her Family,* Harriet Preston, St. Joseph, 1984.
Civil War years in St. Joseph.

Rakstis, Ted, *By the Waters: Benton Harbor Centennial, 1866-1966*, Benton Harbor Centennial Association, 1966.
Centennial program and picture album.

Reber, L. Benjamin, *History of St. Joseph,* St. Joseph Chamber of Commerce, 1925.

St. Joseph Directory for 1880, Daily News, 1880.
A city directory with a brief history of St. Joseph and descriptions of some local businesses.

Schultz, Robert E., *Twin Cities Trolleys: A History of Street Railways and Interurbans in Benton Harbor and St. Joseph, Michigan*, Robert E. Schultz, Las Vegas, Nevada, 1984.

Spencer, Ruth Robbins, *The Higman Park Story 1905-1973*, Ruth Robbins Spencer, Benton Harbor.

Sterling, Anthony, *King of the Harem Heaven,* Monarch Books, Derby, Connecticut, about 1960.
Popular paperback story of the House of David.

Watt, Marilyn, *We'll Hail and Remember,* St. Joseph *Herald-Press,* 1944 and 1945, ed. A. G. Preston, Jr., St. Joseph, 1986.
Biographical sketches of some well-known St. Joseph people of the 1940s.

Webster, Mildred E. and Krause, Fred, *French St. Joseph: Le Poste de la Riviere, St. Joseph 1690-1780,* George Johnson Graphics, Decatur, Michigan, 1986.

Barbara G. Troost is an assistant at the Maud Preston Palenske Memorial Library.